FORE! PLAY

FORE! PLAY

The Last American Male
Takes up Golf

Bill Geist

WARNER BOOKS

A Time Warner Company

Warner Books, Inc., 1271 Avenue of the Americas, New York, NY 10020
Visit our Web site at www.twbookmark.com

 A Time Warner Company

Printed in the United States of America
First Printing: April 2001
10 9 8 7 6 5 4 3 2 1

Library of Congress Cataloging-in-Publication Data

Geist, William.
    Fore! play : the last American male takes up golf / Bill Geist.
       p. cm.
    ISBN 0-446-52763-7
       1. Golf—Anecdotes. 2. Golf—Humor. I. Title.

GV967 .G45 2001
796.352'02'07—dc21

                                                                    00-066256

Book design by Giorgetta Bell McRee

ACKNOWLEDGMENTS

Thanks, as always and for everything, to Jody, Libby, and Willie, for playing along. Thanks to Tom Connor for getting me into another fine mess, and to Rick Wolff, a great editor and a bad golfer who understands. Special thanks to my partners, John McMeel, Pat Oliphant, and John O'Day of the Bad Golfers Association. Thanks to Liz Kloak, my teacher; to Val Ramsdell and others for putting their country club memberships on the line to take me golfing; to Brian, my brave caddy; to Dr. Phil Lee, my golf therapist; to Herb Sambol and Chip Bechert at Metedeconk National Golf Club; to Madeline Cassano at the Paramus Golf Course; to Jerry and Peg Brennan of Grandpa Brennan's Previously Owned Golf Ball Emporium; to Reg Petersen, Golf Ball King; to all the folks at Goat Hill; to Jack Batman and Brad Fazzone at Chelsea Piers; to Rod Tomlinson, Andy Stewart, and Bob Andrews of the U.S. Blind Golf Association; Leslie

Acknowledgments

Bennison; partners Bert Webbe, Billy Dunn, and Dave Councilor; officials and entrepreneurs at the PGA Golf Merchandise Show; Jim Duncalf, the genius behind the Ballistic Driver; and thanks as always to the good people at the AmEx billing department for their unrelenting monthly motivation.

CONTENTS

INTRODUCTION:

How Green Is My Fairway?

"I was up and down, but she lipped out on me."
"Hit it dead, but no bite."
"Shanked it with Bertha."
"Chili-dipped the son-of-a-bitch, didn't catch the apron, and rolled right into the pot bunker."

What are these people *saying?* I might as well be at a cocktail party in Kuala Lumpur with people speaking Bahasa.

But we're in suburban America, and they're talking golf. I don't understand the language, but lately sense I'd better learn it now that we're living in an occupied nation of golfers. Berlitz needs to start offering Golf.

It's becoming a universal language (Esperanto had its chance) here on Planet Golf, where the game is now played and spoken everywhere. It's not just for

Republicans anymore. *Commies* play golf! I've seen the new bourgeois golf resort in Cuba (first new course since the revolution) and seen historic photographs of Castro and Che Guevara playing in their fatigues! I've watched Russians picnicking on the greens and fishing in the water hazards at the first country club in Moscow, thinking it was a park. I've seen sober Japanese golfers playing in the snow—and drunken Minnesotans, too.

Is there golf as we know it elsewhere in the universe? Yes. In an attempt to avoid exorbitant greens fees here on earth, astronaut Alan Shepard smuggled a golf club and some balls aboard Apollo 14 and teed off on the moon. Wearing that bulky space suit caused him to whiff a couple of times, but on his third try the shot carried for "miles and miles and miles."

"Hit the 7 fat on 8, the 9 thin on 10."

"I skull my third, goes OB, take a drop, I'm lying 5."

I know all these people discussing their skulling and chili-dipping and shanking. They never used to talk like this. We used to tell jokes together, and talk about politics and celebrities and *Saturday Night Live* and what complete asses our kids' coaches were. Lately, it's like we've never known each other. They've been *taken* by golf, like something out of *Invasion of the Body Snatchers*, Pod People in golf spikes.

Has someone programmed them not to speak of Other Things? Everything relates to golf: "Lung cancer, Jim? Hope it's not affecting your golf game." They go on golf safaris to Kenya and all they have to say when they get back is that the greens were fast and you got a free drop if you hit into a hippo track.

They drone on and on about their latest round (golfers who can barely come up with their children's names can recall in detail every shot they ever took), and for variety tell golf jokes: "So his partner says, 'No, 65 isn't my score, it's my handicap!'" Hahaha. Then they leave the party prematurely so they can get home and read *The Tao of Putting* and articles in *Golf* magazine ("Getting More Trunk Rotation") before hitting the sack early to make that sunrise tee time. They like to play early so they can get home in time to watch golf on TV all afternoon.

I am always left out on the periphery of these golfers' party huddles, usually in about the third row, a wallflower. Eventually I'll wander away, over to the womenfolk, who could always be counted upon for interesting conversation in the old days when men were going on and on about the stock market and their kids' athletic prowess. No more. These days, women tend to be talking about their golf lessons or the golf camp a dozen of them will be attending next week in North Carolina—talk that's interesting only when they describe the advances made by lesbian instructors.

My dentist plays five times a week except in the dead of winter. Five! At my June appointment, his assistant is cleaning my teeth, when he breezes in, checks me over for about, oh, forty-five seconds, says, "You have a good-looking set of teeth there," and is out the door for the links.

"Wungee gar-ngh glff gnugs?" I ask the dental hygienist, who takes the equipment out of my mouth so I can repeat the question: "Weren't those *golf* gloves he was wearing when he examined me?"

The dentist says he offers reduced rates on rainy days,

and was far more attentive at my winter appointment when it was sleeting. He took me into his office, which is something of a shrine to golf, his shelves lined with photographs of him and his family at golf courses home and abroad, his walls covered with oil paintings of golf holes.

"This one is at Pine Valley," he says reverently, referring to the New Jersey course that's sacred ground to golfers, a reference lost on me. "See that bunker there," he says, pointing to a sand trap in the painting. "You know what they call that?" I do not, unaware that sand traps are to be called bunkers and that they have proper names. "They call it 'The Devil's Asshole.' "

He practices his swing there in the office between patients with a special club that's weighted to build golf muscles and shortened to prevent breaking lamps. On the way out, I tell his receptionist to please cancel any of my future appointments after he's had a bad round. Could there be anything worse than an angry golfer with a dentist drill?

Golf fever. It's serious, it's viral, it's epidemic, and unlike West Nile no one is spraying for it. There are now 26.4 million golfers in America playing on 16,743 courses and unable to stop. (The American Association of Retired Persons reports, however, there are 67 million Americans over fifty and that fully 67 million of them play golf—which seems an underestimate when you try to play a course in Florida or try to get into a Sizzler for the Early Bird Special at 4:00 P.M.)

It's an addiction, "upper-middle-class crack," says my friend Art, who's become totally hooked. It can become problematic when devotees ignore jobs and spouses, al-

4

though many of the golfers I know are at points in their careers and have been married so long that they can comfortably do both without any repercussions. You don't see a lot of "golf widows" weeping on *Oprah*; most of them are glad to get their guy out of the house for a while.

Another friend, Mike, plays constantly, sometimes thirty-six holes a day. He plays in the rain, of course, but he also plays in the snow, glueing colorful little tails to the balls so he can see them. But it's worse than that. Mike has been known to play at *night* with glow-in-the-dark golf balls.

The epidemic is not without historical precedent. This game, which goes back to Roman times and to Scottish shepherds hitting stones into holes with sticks, was outlawed in 1457 by Scotland's King James I because people were fooling around playing golf when they should have been practicing their archery for the national defense. Way before the LPGA, Mary Queen of Scots became so addicted that when in 1567 she was informed on the golf course of the murder of her husband she went ahead and finished the round. That incident was cited as evidence of her coldheartedness when she was tried for treason and beheaded—to this day the most severe golf penalty ever handed down. Most infractions still just cost you a stroke.

Another friend of mine spends a good deal of time these days designing golf holes on his computer—as a hobby. There are plastic model kits of golf holes that grown men build. Some people we know have those oil paintings of golf holes, and little golfer figurines, and display cases of golf balls hanging on their walls. Some subscribe to the twenty-four-hour Golf Channel. Some go to the twenty-four-hour golf course on Long Island. There are folks in the area installing putting greens in their backyards. Shaquille O'Neal has one in his front yard. Some people are installing entire golf courses in their yards, like the Internet zillionaire near Palo Alto who bought three neighboring houses for $4.5 million and had a demolition party—where guests got to drive the bull-dozers!—to clear some room so he could build a golf course.

Although my golfing friends tend to be otherwise smart, successful people, they will buy anything any TV huckster suggests will lower their handicaps. You think those people transfixed by Jerry Springer and ordering in-fomercial gadgets that scramble eggs inside the shells are idiots? They are, of course, but how about guys with MBAs ordering herbal golf *pills* to improve their games?

Why? What is it about this sport? *Is* it a sport? I mean are there teams? Uniforms? Stadiums? Coaches? Cheerleaders? Hot dogs and beer? Bench-clearing brawls? Any of that stuff they have in real sports like base-ball, basketball, football, hockey, and soccer?

Golf is different, maybe more like genteel tennis, except in golf there isn't even an *opponent*. And the ball doesn't move. That would make it harder, if someone sort of rolled the ball at the golfer as he swung at it. So golf does-n't require that advanced degree of hand-eye coordination exactly. Nor strength, agility, speed, or quickness. It's more like Chinese checkers in that regard, and perhaps most akin to bowling—but no golfer wants to admit *that*. Bowling with landscaping.

It's not a "Higher-Faster-Stronger" classic Olympic sport either. The Greeks never played golf. Golf isn't in the Olympics at a time when almost everything conceivable and inconceivable *is*. I mean ballroom dancing may be in the next Olympics. C'mon!

Now, my golfing bears a strong resemblance to the new, emerging sport of orienteering (also trying to get into the Olympics), as I'm always walking around looking for my ball, lost in the woods, trying to figure out which way it might be to the green and which fairway I'm currently on.

No other sport has par. Why is there par? And it's the only one where low score wins. No other sport has so many different implements—and caddies to carry them and follow players around making suggestions. What if Michael Jordan had a guy running up and down the court with him, saying: "I'd use the crossover dribble here, and since you drove to the hoop last time, I'd pull up and drain the three."

And Michael certainly would have done a helluva lot better without anyone guarding him. Golf has no *defense!*

Golf is the only sport where you have to bring your own ball, the only sport with etiquette primers, and the only one with *handicaps!* Let's see, with that five-run handicap the Cubs win again! Better make it six.

It's the only one where the players keep their own scores. Imagine if quarterbacks Kurt Warner and Peyton Manning met at the fifty-yard line after a big football playoff game as a packed stadium tensely looked on:

"What's your scorecard look like, Kurt?"

"Well, Peyton, I put myself down for a touchdown and extra point in the first quarter, another 7 in the second, 14 in the third, and 21 in the fourth for 49 points. But I did take a mulligan—five downs—on that last touchdown pass."

"Gee, Kurt, that's okay. Counting that 15-yard gimmee field goal I have a 45, so it looks like you win."

And Rams fans go wild!

In golf, fans don't go wild. They have to be quiet most of the time. When something good happens there is polite applause, the kind you hear after the guest speaker on "Transplanting Delphiniums" at the garden club.

Announcers *whisper*, like they're broadcasting a church service or reference work at the library. They say that fans and announcers must be quiet because golfers have to concentrate. Yeah, like basketball players don't have to concentrate to sink a fourth-quarter foul shot while hundreds of screaming fans wave colorful three-foot polystyrene weenies behind the basket.

So golf seems less a sport than an *activity*, even though it borders a good deal of the time on inactivity. How does golf stack up against napping? Napping is preferred by many because there are no lessons, skills, frustrations, complex rules, outfits, expensive tools, fees, and special shoes—although it would not surprise me if Nike came out with $100 napping shoes.

Moreover, golf is a noncontact, nonaerobic activity—although personally I get more exercise than most, hitting the ball nearly twice as many times as my partners and walking many more miles in my serpentine paths to the greens. Still, it requires much the same conditioning as stamp collecting. Running is not permitted on the golf course.

It is also a *game,* a game of great skill and practice. One that frustrates great athletes like Michael Jordan and very good athletes like my son and formerly mediocre athletes like myself. It is written that two thirds of new golfers give it up after five years. Golf even frustrates Tiger. Watch him shake his head and mutter all day on his way to another championship.

So what draws these hundreds of millions? What attracts Bill Clinton and Celine Dion and John Updike and Alice Cooper and Hootie and the Blowfish?

Updike writes (Cooper does not): "As it moves through a golf match the human body, like Alice in Wonderland, experiences intoxicating relativity—huge in relation to the ball, tiny in relation to the course, exactly matched to that of the other players. From this relativity is struck a silent music that rings to the treetops and runs through a Wagnerian array of changes as each hole evokes its set of shots, dwindling down to the final putt. The clubs in their nice gradations suggest organ pipes."

Huh? So, as we were saying, what draws people to golf?

Many things. It is the only sport with carts and cocktails. I'd still play basketball if you could use carts. When you're young, you play baseball, basketball, soccer, and other games where the ball moves and so do you. As you get older you either play doubles tennis, where *you* don't move, or golf, where the ball doesn't. Or you watch others play these games on TV.

I predict that sumo wrestling will become the next big sport for aging baby boomers, because it actually *requires* participants to be fat and it usually lasts about three seconds. Golf is currently the only sport in which fat, middle-aged chain-smokers can flat out kick your butt. It is also the only one that offers any hope of improvement to these out-of-shape athletes, if you will, over fifty.

Another reason people play golf is what I shall call here the "Ice Fishing Factor," which holds that men will do almost *anything* to get away from their loved ones for a while—to include sitting in a shed on a frozen lake all day drinking syrupy schnapps and looking at a hole in the ice.

Another reason is that like trout fishing, golf takes place in beautiful places, many as lavishly landscaped as Japanese gardens; pastoral, serene enclaves offering a few hours of escape from the hustle and bustle, from traffic, from television, even from cell phones, which are banned at many clubs—reason enough to play golf.

Golf confers a measure of class on its players, smacking of the idle rich. One must be of a certain station in life to take off four or five hours on a Tuesday afternoon to play golf. Not to mention joining an exclusive golf club. Show me the Winged Sphere National Bowling Club that costs $50,000 to join and where a single blackball can keep prospective members off the lanes.

Golf is good for business, my friends tell me. But in my case it would probably be the medical business, the personal injury law business, the window replacement business—as well as golf ball sales.

They proselytize, these golfers, worse than the Jehovah's Witnesses. A friend came to the door to give me a golf magazine featuring an article on why everyone should take up golf and I felt like he'd handed me *Lamp Unto My Feet*.

They always ask me to play with them, saying, incorrectly, that I couldn't possibly be as bad as I claim to be. They say it doesn't even matter if I'm bad, so long as I just keep hitting the ball and don't hold them up.

They speak of the fragrance of freshly mown grass, of the sparkle of the morning dew, of fawns scampering across the fairways, of the exhilaration of hitting even one fine shot, of relaxation and serenity, and, perhaps most of all, of the camaraderie.

I can't argue with any of that. I've had terrific times out on golf courses on beautiful days with partners who could hit bad shots and laugh about them. It's just the damned frustrating, maddening, impossible, merciless game I hate.

But I want to see my friends and about the only place to do that anymore is on a golf course.

So, I'm giving it a try. But I'm not going to call it a "try," I'm calling it "one man's personal journey" so maybe I can attract a little interest from Oprah's Book Club. I approach this with some hesitation, steeling myself for humiliation, and fearing addiction.

I mean these golf nuts are gone, folks. Round the bend. And they're not coming back. I have friends who are plopping down $1,500 or more for clubs, $50,000 to join the country club, taking golf vacations to California and Scotland, and moving to golf communities so they can literally *live* on the golf course (and have my golf balls land on their coffee tables). There are coffins decorated in golf motifs.

Now, if golf were a religious cult, and I certainly don't mean to imply it isn't, and you saw your friends suddenly

11

acting in such an irrational fashion, you'd have them *de-programmed!*

And if someone like Chi Chi Rodriguez should take them on a golf vacation to Guyana and tell them they are all going to a better place, the big country club in the sky, where there are no monthly food minimums and they will play par golf with custom Callaway clubs on a Robert Trent Jones–designed course every day for all of eternity . . . what do you think happens?

They drink the Kool-Aid, no question.

1

A Life in the Rough

I am from a golf-deprived background. No one taught me to play. I picked up the game in the 1950s on the hardscrabble streets of my hometown, Champaign, Illinois, first in my own yard where my brother Dave sank a number of tin cans, then at a miniature golf course across from a trailer park, and finally at a little 9-hole public course between a cemetery and a pigpen.

Of the two forms of golf, little and big, I preferred the mini version, where there was always a lot of laughing, and where a really bad shot—one that hit another golfer or another golfer's Buick, or one that skittered across the street and had to be played out of the Illini Pest Control parking lot—was always considered the very best shot of the day. It takes a certain skill to get some loft on the ball and drive it that far with a putter.

We played (for 35 cents, as I recall) on warm summer nights, the course semilit by dim bulbs strung here and

13

there, accompanied by the sounds of crickets and top ten tunes like "Green Door" or "Tammy" that were trying to make themselves heard on the single raspy speaker attached to the shack. The balls were colorful and the clubs almost dangerously barbed and ratty, having the look and feel of spoons that had been dropped into a garbage disposal—except those weren't invented yet. There were always friends there, and sometimes a group of cute girls in short shorts that would cause my friends and me to show off—sometimes in ways that involved minor property damage and expulsion.

It was exotic. There was the little bowed bridge over a six-by-eight-foot pond—probably the largest body of water in the county. And there was the windmill. How clever. Turns out all mini-golf courses have windmills, but I didn't know that. We didn't get around much. Provincial? Our high school foreign exchange student was from America. Hawaii. Who knew?

Mini-golf was fun. But big golf is not played for fun per se. You don't hear a lot of laughing on your standard-sized courses. Oh, there was some laughing at that public 9-hole course, where players were generally awful, not serious about the game, sometimes drunk, sometimes without any golfing equipment, and occasionally there just to make out. You never see couples making out on the country club course or at those golf tournaments on TV. Too bad.

My friends and I didn't know how to play, and we didn't know that the 9-hole course was as bad as we were. A round of golf cost next to nothing and that seemed a fair price. Actually, I'm not sure we paid. I think if you started on the second tee you didn't have to pay.

The course had no landscaping as such: no trees, no berms, no sand traps, no rough—just the tees, straight fairways, and flat little greens. Like a sod farm. On one fairway, the designer decided to get a little tricky, placing across its width a foot-high, grass-covered hurdle that resembled an enlarged speed bump—although in retrospect that might have been a sewer pipe or the work of a large rodent.

That was all to the good. We were not accustomed to trees—all of which had been wiped out by Dutch elm disease—or topographical aberrations like slopes, knolls, or knobs—let alone hills. We were flatlanders. The land was flat in every direction for hundreds of miles. My driveway was the steepest slope in town. The first time I saw hills and curves, I rolled my Volkswagen.

I inherited my golf clubs from an uncle killed in World War II. There were four in the bag as I recall: two putters, a driver, and an iron. My friends and I approached the game as just an enlarged version of miniature golf, really. We just swung harder and were pleasantly surprised to find there were no windmills to take into account on the greens. We played poorly, were uninterested in improvement, and laughed at ourselves and others. Unfortunately, this was to become our overall philosophy of life. We approached everything the same way. When we bowled at the fabulous new automated Arrowhead Lanes, we imitated the mannerisms, nuances, and seriousness of TV bowlers, while depositing balls in the gutters. We filched the green, red, and tan bowling shoes with the sizes displayed on the backs, and wore them to school. The fad never caught on.

I don't know that we kept score on that golf course. When you start on the second tee, you don't get a score-card. Par was probably three for each hole on the course, although I'm sure a good pro could do them all in two, with no hazards, other than the police, who were occasionally summoned when there were, say, fifty golfers on the course and no gate receipts. Our scores were probably in the 60s, respectable on the pro tour, not so hot on a par-3 9-holer.

It was here I developed my pronounced hook shot (something I never could do in bowling) and my noteworthy ability to play amongst tombstones. If your hook was severe, you could hit a drive into the cemetery, where my grandfather was buried. You had to hit for distance, though, to clear the street and the hedgerow. I did that only once, with the assistance of a strong crosswind, and I did have to go look for the ball because I could only afford the one. After paying my respects at the family grave site, I advanced my ball several plots with my iron, before electing to throw the ball back in play rather than trying to chip it over the hedge and the street. It was a decent toss (I played pitcher and third base as a kid), but still short of the green, leaving me two chip shots and four putts before holing out.

A slice on that course could be even worse. The course was positioned—as are so many things in the Midwest— next to pig and cattle pens, and a severely sliced shot could mean wading through animal dung (actual bull-shit!) to play your ball. If it were actually in actual bull-shit, what to do? Pick it up? With what? Try to hit it out?

This may be where the term "chip shot" was coined, I don't know.

For all the golfers playing the course, not just the ones bad enough to hit *into* the pens, a southerly breeze through that area turned a round of golf into a memorable odoriferous experience. Ever try to putt and gag at the same time?

The first real golf outing I can remember was with a group of former college buddies a couple of years after we'd all graduated, on a weekend with our wives at a house on Lake Michigan.

Most of them had played golf throughout college. And bridge. I didn't play golf or bridge because my older brother played bridge and suffered from a dangerously low grade point average as a result. I didn't want to become hooked on those vices. So I began playing pinball machines on occasion and then for several hours every day. For five years (had the two senior years). We didn't have carpal tunnel syndrome back then or I would have died from it.

On our outing, we left the house in the morning and didn't return until early evening, the great length of time owing to the number of strokes I required as well as to the vast amount of time I spent hunting for my ball.

I have tried to block out memories of that golf outing, but I do occasionally have flashbacks. Frankly, I prefer the flashbacks to 'Nam. I was in a kind of Jerry Lewis mode that day and there were a lot of laughs, all at my expense.

I recall having a golf bag slung over my shoulder, not like you're supposed to, with the clubs low and by your side, but rather with the clubs riding high behind my right shoulder like soldiers carry rifles. At any rate, when I bent forward to tee up my ball, all of the clubs fell out, cascading over the top of my head. That one had them rolling on the fairways.

I also recall stroking a ball and having a golf cart whir up behind me with a man shouting: "Hey, you just hit my ball!"

"No," I said, "I think I've been playing the Jim Jeffries brand ball all along."

"I *am* Jim Jeffries," he replied. I was unaware golfers sometimes had their names stamped on their balls.

It was on this day, too, that I performed a truly miraculous golf feat that defies both belief and the fundamental laws of physics. Let's just say if Jesus had done it (at Bethlehem Hills Country Club) they'd be teaching the tale in Sunday School.

I teed up the ball, and of course everyone in my group was staring at me, because they didn't want to miss something good. What they saw they will likely never see again.

I took a healthy backswing, whipped the driver through, and did manage to strike the ball, rather than pounding the turf behind it or going over the top and completely whiffing as is so often the case. My partners gazed down-range, but could not pick up the flight of the ball. About two seconds after my swing there was a dull thud as it came to earth not more than twenty feet from the tee.

Behind the tee! I had hit my drive backward, apparently stroking it almost straight up but with so much backspin that it landed behind me. This time my friends did not immediately laugh. They were dumbstruck . . . aghast . . . awed at that to which they had borne witness.

That was in the early 1970s. Since then I have continued to amuse others by playing my own quixotic brand of golf in which I keep striving to reach the unreachable par. For fifty years I have played pretty much Par Free Golf.

2

Possibly the Last American Male Takes Up Golf

Ten people scurry around the small gym, chasing little plastic balls bouncing off the walls. It sort of resembles handball . . . a little bit . . . maybe team handball . . . played with big teams . . . and golf clubs . . . and lots of little hollow balls with holes in them. And mayhem. It closely resembles mayhem.

The little game begins with ten people lined up in the middle, five of them facing one wall and five facing the opposite wall. They stroke the plastic balls at the walls with 9-irons, then scramble all over the place trying to re-trieve the rebounds careening this way and that. When the balls ricochet straight back, the players look like hockey goalies trying to make saves.

What *is* this? This is bizarre, that's what. This is my golf class. On a Monday night in February, with the tem-perature 28 degrees outside, here we are trying to learn to play golf inside an elementary school gym in New Jersey.

Can this actually *happen?*

I've signed up for a community school night class, which is not exactly a week at Pebble Beach in the Jack Nicklaus Golf Academy, but it's a start. And, it's sixty-nine bucks! For six lessons. And that includes your own personal carpet swatch, which you place on the floor to hit the balls from—although sometimes my particular carpet sample travels farther than the ball.

"Whoa!" exclaims the instructor, Liz Kloak, when the bad golf genie makes my little rug fly. "Watch it there."

All the students are saying their "I'm sorry"s as they run in front of each other chasing their balls. Or their "Oh! I'm Really Sorry!"s as their mis-struck balls strike fellow students. It could be worse. The balls could be real. Liz says a student in a previous class didn't quite "get it," and hit a real ball that came back and struck another student in the foot. Luckily, the victim worked for Johnson & Johnson and had bandages in her car.

Our motley group is clearly not ready for hoity-toity golf schools anyway, and is better off by far in the capable, compassionate hands of Liz, who loves golf as it was gently taught to her by her kindly father. She's a great golfer, but as a mother of three who's six months pregnant ("my stomach is costing me fifteen yards on my drive"), she has some perspective, always saying reasonable, comforting words to us like "It's just a game" and "So, don't keep score."

She also has a great Boston—"Bahstan"—accent: "Do it this way and you'll get mo-ah yahdage and a bettah chance at pah." Students occasionally ask for a translation.

21

"Look at the ball!" she bellows, but amiably, at a student whose carpet is scooting across the gym.

"Don't try to kill it!" she hollers to a guy who has swung as hard as he can and has missed the ball entirely.

"Face the direction you want to hit it," she admonishes a cockeyed student.

That would seem obvious, but this is your basic instruction. A class for rank beginners. "Say you're a 'novice,' " Liz suggests. "It sounds better than 'beginner' and doesn't scare the golfers around you as much."

Students in her two back-to-back evening classes range in age from eleven years old to sixty-seven. Six men and five women in the first seventy-five-minute class, nine women and one man in the second. There are couples taking up golf together, women who want to take it up for business reasons, other women who want to be able to play golf with their husbands because that's the only way they'll ever see them, still other women who think they might meet rich men on the golf course, men who are giving up on more strenuous sports, and men and women alike who just think golf looks like fun. "I don't take it too seriously," says Michelle, hitting one sideways. "I can be miserable at home."

We don't even know how to hold a club, so Liz starts with the grip. Unfortunately, four of us are out of town for that first class. The next week she works on the swing. Unfortunately, the four of us have not been notified that the class has been relocated, so we meet at the wrong location for Class No. 2 and shoot the breeze for twenty minutes before figuring out there's a problem and heading home. Now, we'll only have four classes to learn golf.

"I told you we should have taken Tiger Schulmann's karate class," one of our estranged foursome says to her friend. These two are taking the class together—to learn golf, yes, but also to get the hell out of the house one night a week. The friend doesn't seem to mind at all that she's wasting time at the wrong location missing golf class, "just so I get home after the kids are in bed. Let's go over to Finnegan's [bar] for a drink."

At Class No. 3, Liz gives the four of us a quick course in the grip: "Your left hand is your rudder. Your thumb goes straight down the shaft. Grip it firmly but don't white-knuckle it. Your right hand can be rotated clockwise or counterclockwise slightly to adjust your shot. Clockwise opens your grip to stop hooking . . . the opposite to stop slicing." Got it? Okay.

She speeds ahead. "Now, in your stance your feet are shoulder width wide, your knees are bent, with all joints relaxed. Keep your head down and swing slowly. Get over that kill thing. If you swing hard and fast you don't hit it squarely. Hitting the sweet spot generates power. That's why 120-pound women can hit it three-hundred yards. Do not accelerate on the downswing. For more distance just take it back farther. Same tempo up and back. Count 1-2-3 up and 1-2-3 down like a pendulum if you have to."

Slow down. Bring your left shoulder into your sight plane on the backswing, then bring your right shoulder into your sight plane. My mother wears purple so she sees her shoulders. "And finish. Throw the club over your shoulder—no, *gently*, or you'll break your neck—on your follow-through. And when it's a good shot, stand there with that club over your shoulder and admire it in a pose for a minute, like this, even if it annoys your partners. My husband always has to tell me 'that's enough!' "

Okay-okay-okay-I've-just-heard-more-about-golf-in-five-minutes-than-I've-been-told-in-fifty-years. But how can you possibly remember to do all those good things at once? Yogi Berra said "You can't think and hit a baseball at the same time," and for once he made sense.

There's a lot to learn when you've picked up your swing from watching highway maintenance crews cutting weeds along the interstate. This will take time. More than I have left here on the firmament, unfortunately.

The four of us join the group and begin to hit our first balls. "Generate loft!" Liz instructs a student who is on his hands and knees the whole class searching for the balls he's firing under the pile of tumbling mats in the corner. "Launch, don't push."

One student disappears for ten minutes and finally walks out from behind the curtain on the stage, where he's lost a few balls. I'm thinking that if we're losing balls in this little gym it does not bode well for us in the great outdoors—which is quite vast.

Indeed, Liz cautions: "If you hook it or slice it here, you're really going to hook it and slice it on the course."

Halfway through the seventy-five-minute class, one woman has yet to hit the gym wall, which is a large target just twenty feet away. On that wall hangs a poster of Cal Ripkin staring back at her. Below Cal's picture in six-inch-high letters is the word "Perseverance."

"Remember, bad shots tell you more than good shots," she says encouragingly as I hit a ball sideways. In my case I think they might be telling me to leave.

"It should feel natural," Liz says, standing behind a woman with her arms wrapped around her, going through the swinging motion.

"Nothing feels natural," replies the woman, who unfortunately disappeared from class after two weeks.

"You're grimacing," Liz says to the next student. "Are you in pain? Golf is not meant to be physically painful. It is meant to be emotionally painful." All agree that it certainly is.

"How many went to the driving range over the weekend like I suggested?" Liz asks. "None? Well it's a little cold. Remember, at the range, don't stand too near to the ones you love. Balls fly all over the place. And if the experience is a nightmare, change clubs."

A couple of students in the second class say they did go to the range, but with mixed results. The mother of the eleven-year-old in class, Sean, says she went to the driving range and that she's hitting the ball straighter now—but only fifty yards.

"With which club?" Liz asks.

"All of them" is the reply.

"Where's Sean tonight?" the teacher asks.

"He had homework," his mother replies.

"Tiger Woods never had homework," comments another student.

"What if you're missing the ball completely?" asks another.

"You're probably swinging hard and fast and not looking at the ball and pulling your head up," Liz answers.

One woman says she slices, and Liz tells her: "Women tend to slice more. We push the ball instead of striking it,

25

and we don't follow through." Women like myself. Liz tells me to make sure my thumbs are straight, then rotate my right hand counterclockwise, close the clubface, and "finish!" Previously, my approach was to look at the hole, turn my body 45 degrees to the left, and hit my normal slice. The trouble is that when you do it that way, the ball does what it's never done before: goes straight.

Another student says her problem is that she hooks all the time. "As long as your bad shots still have names," Liz says without a trace of irony. "Slices and hooks we can try to deal with."

The topic of the next class is: "The Pitch," which I thought might be a lesson in how to cheat by pitching— i.e., throwing—the golf ball baseball-style. When I attended the University of Missouri, a guy there set a world record that apparently still stands for 18 holes played by throwing the golf ball, an 84.

"The pitch is used for shots less than a hundred yards," Liz tells us. What I don't tell her is that *all* my shots are less than a hundred yards. I can only *drive* the ball a hundred yards. "You'll use your 9-iron or maybe the 8, or the one that says P for pitch on it."

I wasn't sure what those letters on the clubs stood for. Or the numbers either for that matter. I didn't know the 1 was the driver until a couple weeks ago. I thought the P might mean it was strictly for Poor or possibly Piss-Poor shots, which were all I ever hit with it.

She demonstrates by hitting the ball perfectly, off the center of the basketball backboard. She once took an entire class outside the school, where she demonstrated a 5-

wood shot that was all too perfect, traveling over a house at the end of the baseball field. A policeman returned the ball—the evidence. "The officer was impressed with the distance," Liz says in all modesty. "The truth is, I now know how far all my clubs will hit the ball." Imagine. She even has an idea of what direction.

After her perfect backboard shot, we take over, hacking and thwacking the balls—and the little carpets—every which way. I hear the young woman next to me complain "I can't do this shot"—and she isn't kidding. But when she repeats herself I realize that, no, she isn't saying "I can't do this shot"; what she's saying is "I can't do this shit," referring not simply to this particular piddling little shot, but to "All This Shit," meaning the entire game of golf.

Appropriately enough, our next lesson is on the S club. No, the S stands for sand wedge. "You will be in the sand a lot at first," Liz warns, but remains positive. "At least in a sand trap you can still see your ball. It's not in the woods or underwater." She tells us that an S does not always come with a set of clubs, but to be sure to buy one because we'll be needing it. Badly.

"Now on a New Jersey public course," she continues, "the sand is going to be different than at a nice private course in Florida, where it's dry and fine. Here it's heavy, wet, rocky, muddy New Jersey muck. And you'll have to swing harder."

"And oh yeah," she adds. "After you've swung three times unsuccessfully, pick up your ball and leave. But remember to rake the sand. In golf, etiquette is very important."

She says if we are polite and not slow we will be welcome to play anywhere, despite being bad.

"It should only take four to four and a half hours to play," she says.

"You mean for 9 holes," says a student, speaking from experience.

"Nooo," says Liz, patiently, "that would be for the full 18."

After putting class, we take up scoring, which is something of a sore subject with this group. Liz's first piece of advice is: "Once you've doubled par, pick up your ball and move on for the sake of golfers behind you. It's just not that important if you get a 13 instead of a 14."

Liz defines terms like "eagle."

"Why would we need to know that?" a student asks. Good question. Occasionally we have to remind Liz how bad we are, like when she starts telling us that a red flag means the hole is on the front of the green, or how to toss grass to gauge windage, or reading yardage marks on sprinkler heads. We really don't have much use for that kind of detailed information.

Liz tells us of birdies, pars, bogeys, double bogeys, and more useful terms like triple bogey, which is something we can certainly all shoot for. Other useful terms include colorful phrases like "snowman," which is an 8, and "picket fence," which sounds like an 11.

Naturally, students bring up cheating as a way to improve their scores. Liz doesn't condone putting down a 6 when you shoot an 8, but admits that partners may not catch you or call you on it, providing money isn't at stake.

"A true golfer isn't paying attention to *your* shots," she says. "True golfers are only paying attention to their own."

I write that one down. I'll want to use that to admonish any golf partner who accuses me of lying, e.g.: "If you were a *true* golfer you wouldn't even have noticed I shot a 12 instead of a 6!" Bastard.

Her other practical scoring tips include: "A whiff, where you swing and make no contact with the ball, doesn't count." Great news! Although the United States Golf Association disagrees.

Also of immediate help: "If you hit a bad tee shot and the starter's not watching, re-tee and hit again," she advises. "My husband is good at this, very fast. He does it almost every time. He says: 'If you can't afford lots of balls, you shouldn't be playing golf,' and I always say, 'But, George, 18 balls every round?'"

"My husband is always reminding me that he's better and always telling me what to do," a student complains.

"You don't golf with someone so they can tell you what to do," Liz replies. "If you golf as a couple, your husband is only there to tell you where your ball went, to fetch sodas, and to pay."

"Don't *ever* play with your husband!" yells another woman, who has good reason. "The first time we played I was four months pregnant and he wouldn't let me go back and pee. I had to go in the bushes." I jot down a reminder to ask Liz about the rules of urination during our etiquette instruction.

"My husband has an 8 handicap," complains another student, "and I've played three times. It's not fair."

"Well," says Liz, "if he shoots 80 and you shoot 120, take your handicap and tell him you win."

Handicaps are our next class subject. Students are excited. Handicaps may be our only hope. My golf handicap is so high I should get to park in the specially marked spots by the front door at the grocery store. If there was a Special Olympics of golf, I'd be there. At this point they should stop calling it a handicap, and say I'm golf-challenged. Would it kill them to be a little *sensitive?*

Handicaps "level the playing field," as they say, giving me a chance to "beat" anyone on the professional tour. I'm not sure I understand the point. Am I supposed to feel better about my 125?

Handicaps are (almost) enough to make you stop cheating.

"Can we use tees on the fairway?" a student asks.

"No," says Liz, "that's cheating," and then reminds us: "Cheating on your scores will only drive your handicaps down." I'd never thought of it that way. She says some "sandbaggers" will shoot eight pars in a row then purposely shoot a 12 on the next hole to keep their handicaps up. That's getting a little perverted.

However, it does occur to me this might be an excellent excuse for my atrocious golf game. Maybe people will think I'm playing poorly on purpose to keep my handicap up.

Liz says there's great news on the handicap front! "They're giving people 40 and even 45 handicaps, way higher than they used to." Let's see, 45 plus par 72 is . . . well, it's still not quite enough, but in a comprehensive program with some throws and kicks it's going to help a lot.

At the sixth and final class there is real danger. This is the night Liz teaches us how to tee off. Students bring drivers and swing them wild and hard. Diana hits another student in the head with one of her balls. "Medic!" he yells. Jack can't seem to hit the ball with his driver—at all. He whiffs over the top of the ball or he hits the carpet and sends it flying. A couple of times there are thuds and clangs as he hits under or behind the carpet swatch, thwacking the linoleum floor. He may have even produced a linoleum divot on one attempt.

"Take a breath and count to three," Liz says, consoling him. "Keep your chin up but not when you're hitting the ball!"

She instructs another student to stand farther away from the ball with her driver.

"Why?" the student demands to know.

"Because it's longer," Liz replies.

"Don't let your tee shot psych you out," she warns. "It can ruin your whole game. My father taught me to play golf using only a 6-iron. No tee shots. That would be a good idea for you. Just throw that first tee shot if you have to. Or if it gets too bad, just pick up your tee and go."

And with that, school's out for summer. Some of the students stick around to ask individual questions like why pro golfers wiggle their butts and their clubs before hitting the ball, but our golf instruction is over.

Can you really learn to play golf in six hours for sixty-nine bucks in a grade school gym in New Jersey?

Nope. And, to a degree, yes. Liz introduces us to the clubs and to the fundamentals of how to swing them. She succeeds in making us feel like we know enough to at least go out and try to play. And when no one's ever told you anything about the grip or the swing or the clubs or the etiquette, and you find yourself walking out to that first tee, you really do feel a bit like you've been beamed down to an alien planet.

Liz saves her best bit of advice for last: "Don't keep score, not for a long, long time." We turn in our carpet swatches, wish each other luck, and go out into the cold.

3

Bogeyman Goes Public

Christ had an easier time getting up on Easter than I did. Exactly what time *did* he have to rise anyway?

My alarm went off at 5:00 A.M., four hours after I went to bed. I'm not an early riser. Why, I didn't get up till nine in the *army*. True, we lost that one. 'Nam. These days, I've found a job where we don't have to be in the office until ten or ten-thirty. And if any fish out there ever wish to be caught by me, they can damned well wait until noon.

Something they don't tell you when you're learning golf is that you can't actually play! There's no place to do it. There are golf courses everywhere you look in this bountiful land, but they're all jammed. Is there a better reason to support Zero Population Growth and put up electrified fences along our nation's borders? Malthus warned us about this. There are now six billion people on this planet and if we don't get our heads out of the sand we're going to run out of food and tee times!

33

The county I live in has tens of thousands of golfers registered to play at three public courses, and Lord knows how many unregistered. Golfers are like dogs in this respect. Indeed it's dog-eat-dog for tee times.

They'll arrive at the Paramus, New Jersey, course at 10:00 P.M. on a Thursday night, for example, so they can be among the first in line at 6:00 A.M. Friday when the sign-up sheet for Saturday tee times is put up. "I used to tell my wife that these people are nuts," one of them named Billy tells me, "and she'd say, 'That's right, they sure are.'"

There's a phone-in reservation system by which you can, theoretically, reserve a tee time seven days in advance. Golfers can call at 12:00:01 A.M. Sunday to reserve a spot for the following Sunday, but by the time their calls go through the course is somehow already booked. The scorned suspect skullduggery.

Regulars do know, however, that there's a raffle over the winter for tee times. My brother-in-law joined a *conglobation* of twelve duffers who entered the raffle for an entire season of tee times. And they won, sort of, if you want to call it that. They won the right to buy twenty-five weekend tee times from April through October for $1,800.

But their allotted tee time was 6:18 A.M.! Moreover, only four of the twelve can play each week, so newcomers like my brother-in-law, Bert, received the less-than-prime dates, such as Father's Day, Mother's Day, and Easter. Some dates are so unpopular that they need substitutes to fill a foursome.

And this is how I am blessed to rise on Easter morning at 5:00 A.M. to play golf. Bert invited me. It is raining. It is 43 degrees. And pitch dark. But we're going, come hell or high water. And in this case we have both.

I put on my golfing attire, such as it is—and a ski parka. And gloves. Not golf gloves. *Winter* gloves. I make a mug of instant coffee, using two tablespoons of coffee and one tablespoon of sugar. At Starbucks, this would be "The Coronary Grande."

I have time to take this strong medicine only because my golf partners arrive five minutes late to pick me up. They had trouble rousing my brother-in-law, and had to mount a Janet Reno–style raid—battering rams, assault weapons—to extract him from bed. His hair resembles the Statue of Liberty's crown when he knocks on my door.

"It's not too bad out," he says. I point to the TV screen where the Weather Channel is telling me it's 43 and raining. "Oh," he replies.

I have a long history of unfortunate experiences with my brother-in-law, some involving sports. He once represented himself as a fisherman, for example, and talked me into going with him on a fishing expedition to Canada, where he implied that trophy fish just jump into your boat. There, too, we arose before dawn on the first day . . . and caught . . . nothing. He looked good, however, donning an Orvis fishing vest and other accoutrements, but it quickly became apparent that he knew not. It is unclear if he knew not that he knew not. He ceremoniously withdrew from his tackle box an antique sterling silver lure from Scotland, tied it to his line, and made his cast . . . a beautiful cast, sailing out and out and . . . "Son-of-a-bitch!" he cried, realizing he'd not tied it securely and the family heirloom was splashing across the waters before

35

plunging to the depths. Gone. Things went from bad to worse. I caught a fish, a northern pike (possibly) that displayed such fearsome fangs Bert insisted on knocking it unconscious before bringing it aboard. As I brought it up, he smacked the fish in the head with a paddle, a glancing blow that knocked it off my line, and we watched it swim away. Hours went by, uneventfully, until we saw a fish swimming in the clear waters directly toward our boat at a depth of less than a foot. Bert again grabbed the paddle and began thwacking the waters, in an attempt to cold-cock the fish. But that approach also failed. And so it went for an entire week until my wife was lucky enough to land a suckerfish.

So, naturally, I am a bit wary about golfing with him. Billy—yes that very aforementioned golf nut—is in my driveway in his minivan. He is the "commissioner" of the twelve-man golf league. It is under his auspices that I'm playing (and so he should be named in any legal actions resulting from the round). With him is Dave, another league member, and as we drive to the course they carry on steady, good-natured banter, the kind of thing I can't stand at such an hour. Turns out these guys like to get up at four and five in the morning. They should get a Dunkin' Donuts franchise.

"This is our first golf outing," Billy says.

"Me, too," I say. "Of my life." They laugh. Why?

"You all have kids?" I ask. They do. "Don't you guys catch a lot of flak at home for not being there on Easter morning for the baskets and church and everything?" They do. Yet . . . they are here. They are golfers.

The sky begins to lighten a bit as we pull into the parking lot at six sharp. And the rain has slowed to a drizzle. I'd hoped for a while that the weather would worsen and we could all go back to bed, but I came to realize that there is no going back with men like these. These men are nuts. Golfers.

We take our bags out of the minivan and head for the clubhouse, which is very nice indeed for a public course. I mean, check out the public basketball and tennis courts sometime, with the bent rims and no nets. Here there's a nice bar, a restaurant, and locker room facilities. It even has a drink cart that runs around the course—unfortunately not at this hour.

Right now the guy behind the desk is saying that due to a computer error we may not have a tee time.

"What's the problem?" Billy asks genially. "We will kill you," I add.

But he finds our reservation and chirps: "And the weather's pretty nice now." Relative to . . . ? He must be from Seattle or Ireland, where they have twenty-six words for rain, and drizzle isn't even one of them. "Drizzle" is one of their words for "nice day."

We head to the first tee, kind of a dead-man-walking situation, except I already feel dead and look forward to playing 18 holes about as much as taking a few thousand volts.

Billy finds some phosphorescent orange cheez–peanut butter crackers still in his bag from last season and graciously offers them to us. And here in the cold and rain of this Easter dawn we partake of the glowing crackers . . . and they're not that bad. I do, however, feel that something is terribly, almost cosmically askew with this whole picture.

Billy is resplendent in a red plaid tam-o'-shanter cap and matching, billowing knickers and long red socks. He'd better be good. Being the commissioner, he dictates that he and I are partners and that I'll receive a two-stroke handicap per hole, Bert one stroke, and he and Dave no handicaps at all. He and Dave, the younger, will walk the course. Bert and I get a cart. My only break of the day, except I can't get the seats to recline.

The custom of making excuses begins. I learn that excuses are a big part of golf: "Sorry I'm not playing my best but I have an inoperable brain tumor today." Common excuses include hangnails, blisters, flulike symptoms, new glasses, and death-of-pet. A lot of guys will limp, and say that six months ago their doctors told them they'd never walk again, let alone play golf. I was watching a golf documentary the other day (yes, I'm becoming one of Them) and it turns out that many golf greats over the years were in horrible accidents where the doctor told them they'd never walk again but each came back to win several championships. Inspiring, yes, but I couldn't help but wonder: Was it the *same* stupid-ass doctor misdiagnosing every case?

Bert complains of a sore wrist, and the compassion flows. We surmise that the sore wrist might have something to do with Bert's date the night before—himself. The candles, the Hungry Man dinner, the single wineglass . . . This pretty much set the tone for empathy and human kindness shown throughout this Easter match.

I have a phobia about the first tee. There are always

other people standing around. I'm a private person. I always close the door when I go to the bathroom, for example, and some might suggest that what I do on a golf course is analogous.

But my first drive is okay. My second shot, however, rolls into a ditch and my third into a sand trap. Not an auspicious beginning. No sense in holding back. I want them to see my complete game. After extricating my ball from the bunker there is a lot of putting, past the hole one way, then back past it the other, pendulum style, with the strokes becoming shorter and shorter until my ball finally plunks down in the hole. I think I had a 7 or 8 on the first—fairly short—hole.

But hey! What chance do we have? It's 43 degrees and drizzling and the Big Guy Upstairs is probably pissed off that we're out here playing golf instead of worshiping Him. I mean, it is *Easter!*

On hole 2, Bert hits into a sand trap. What's worse, it's a sand trap back on hole 1. Dave is already peeing on the bushes. I hit my drive behind a tree and use my first official foot wedge, kicking my ball ever so slightly just so I'm not behind the tree anymore. Bert hits out of the sand trap and his ball lands right near the green. No, not that green. He is in good position for par, but on hole 5. From behind the evergreens we hear him grumbling that he can't find his ball, but he finds someone's and blasts it clear across fairway 2 onto the campus of Bergen Community College, nearby. Fortunately, no students are present on the holiday.

The fact is, the three of us don't really see Bert all that much this day, as he plays on fairways of his own choosing, behind the tree lines. But eventually we all meet up again on the greens, and it's always nice to see him again.

Putting on those greens is a problem. They're soaked and the ball inevitably rolls over a worm or two on the way to the hole. The place is crawling with 'em. In my case, this could help. Anything that throws my putt off-line is all to the good, either as an excuse or as something that might correct its course. There are currently a couple of pounds of mud and worm meat on my cleats. I'm letting it dry for jerky.

On the third hole, Bert's drive comes to rest in a little hole behind and touching a small tree. He could use the foot wedge, but doesn't, a testimony to his character. From here he has to hit the ball left-handed with the back of his iron, an almost impossible shot, as he so demonstrates. Even Dave is struggling, playing over on another fairway. The cart path is missing, perhaps flooded out, and the golf cart becomes an all-terrain vehicle, bouncing in and out of gaping mud holes. Yet somehow, amidst all this, I garner a 6! Which is good. And another 6 on hole 4! With my 2-stroke-per-hole handicap, I actually *win* the hole! This is a Pyrrhic victory since it now makes me fair game for their relentless harassment.

Hole 5 is a par-3, and the other three all put their first drives on the green! It is not a difficult hole. It is a downhill par-3 and Richie, the son of a friend of mine, once hit a grounder hole-in-one here—the only wormburner hole-in-one I've ever heard of.

I do not hit my drive on the green. I opt to hit mine into the sand instead—thick, wet sand, with this huge protruding sod lip—a lip like you see on those tribesmen in

National Geographic with the salad plates inside—hanging out and curling over my ball like a wave on Waikiki beach. I hit the ball, and it in turn hits that big lip, and rolls back into the sand. I hit it again! It hits the lip again, and rolls right back again, and I remember what Liz said about just giving up and picking your ball up at some point, which I finally did. I also remember to call the ball a son-of-a-bitch.

On the green, they've laid the flag way over to one side, a good ten feet away from the line between my ball and the hole. "Is the flag in your way?" Billy asks politely, and they all laugh while I 3-putt.

On the 6th, they harass me even as I try to tee off, a condition that only worsens when I become the only one of us to hit the ball onto the correct fairway. That same level of sportsmanship continues on the green. As Billy lines up his putt with intense concentration, Dave jingles coins in his pocket. Bert drops a club. I drop two clubs just as he swings, and two make infinitely more racket than one. He misses the putt, which is bad because he's my partner. But I am learning the nuances of the game, the kind that are not taught at golf academies.

On 7, a par-4 hole, I somehow make it on the green in 3 strokes. As I line up my putt for what would have been par—par!—Dave drops the flag, and so close by that it almost spears me. I blow the putt. But I tap it in for a 5. A real honest-to-God bogey! I am proud. I see *pros* make bogeys, and just to equal a golf feat that makes Tiger Woods furious makes my day.

On the next hole, Dave steps up his attacks, which is flattering in a way. He purposefully steps on my ball in the fairway, driving it so far down into the soft rain-soaked earth that a backhoe couldn't advance it. When he isn't looking, however, I dig the ball out with my hand and place it on a tee. Bert sees me do it and helpfully suggests that when using tees illegally in the fairway, "always make sure they are green tees." Thank you, Bert.

I notice Dave peeing again, and immediately lodge a protest with the commissioner, asking that he invoke and enforce an arcane golf statute drafted by myself ad hoc stating that players must urinate at least one club length away from the cart path. But it is too late for an injunction this time. Just more "casual water" on a sodden course.

Bert does well on 8, with the advantage of, in essence, having already played this hole. While playing a previous hole, he'd hit two errant shots here on 8, including one from a sand trap. On the fairway, Dave replaces my ball with one that's been sawed in half and I of course don't notice until after I've hit it—and even then it's sort of hard to tell, closely resembling my other shots.

Nine, I don't want to talk too much about. It's 544 yards and I do not hit for any kind of distance. 544? Would there be someplace along the way to stop and rotate the tires on the cart? I begin the long struggle and a mere 7 strokes later reach that far and distant green. Bert plays three fairways to get here. We embrace each other on the green like long-lost friends. He looks older. He is. And I am older than everybody. After a mediocre shot, Billy complains: "That's the trouble with being thirty-four." Thirty-four? I have aftershave—Hai Karate—that's thirty-four.

"We're half done," Billy announces. Half? Three of us go into the clubhouse for strong coffee and to use the bathroom. Dave, you will recall, doesn't need to use the bathroom. Left alone, he proceeds to the 10th tee and hits God-knows-how-many drives he'll not tell us about before he hits one he likes.

Hole 10 is good, in my opinion. I score a 6. Bert hits a fantastic drive, high and deep and this time right down Broadway. "Great shot, Bert," says Billy. "Too bad about that lake."

"What lake?" asks Bert.

"The big one there," says Billy. "I guess you're too short to see it over that little rise."

"This is your course," Bert complains. "You're supposed to tell us about that stuff."

"Oh yeah," says Billy.

On 11, I make another 6 and win the hole outright! I think everyone else had 8s. We don't actually see Bert playing the hole, but we hear a lot of screeching of golf cart tires from behind a berm where he keeps hitting the ball and moving ten feet, hitting the ball and moving ten feet. We worry for a moment there's been a head-on cart collision back there from the sound of things.

A hundred yards beyond the 11th green lies another green on a different course, the adjacent yet worlds apart Ridgewood Country Club. Public golfers have been known to hit one over there and see what it's like to putt on a green that costs more than fifty grand to play.

On 12, Bert hits a particularly bad, short, wood shot, and Billy reminds him, helpfully, that this is not croquet. "Tough love," Billy explains. "It's the only way he'll learn."

This is to be my best hole. A par-3. I hit a relatively bad slice off the tee, which goes to the right of the cart path, hits a tree, and lands in a flower bed behind some sort of . . . house . . . or something. I don't really know what it is, but I do remember from previous experience it's not good to be near dwellings. I hope that maybe the little house is some sort of way station on the course, with Bloody Marys and bathrooms and wood nymphs inside, but it turns out to be a . . . mausoleum. Probably filled with golfers who say things like, "Hey, Bert, this isn't croquet."

The old mausoleum is cool. Better than the obstructions you see on mini-golf courses. I know it's a mausoleum because there is a sign reading: "No Climbing On The Mausoleum." And if I do? Are there specific penalties set forth for Climbing On A Mausoleum?

This mausoleum lies between my ball and the green, and without being able to even see the green, I somehow hit a 9-iron out of the flower bed, through some trees, over the mausoleum, and onto the green about ten feet from the hole. Of course I miss the putt, which comes up one inch short. But one inch from par! Hallelujah!

So, this is golf. One good shot, one good hole, and you gain a measure of confidence. You think maybe you have momentum, you think perhaps you're "in the zone"—but, of course, you are not.

And so it is that on the next hole—13—I drive a nasty slice into the trees, producing a clear, crisp, honest KNOCK! Somehow, it is pleasant to the ear. My next shot hits high in another tree and drops a good hundred feet straight down on the cart path, bouncing straight back up and, not to brag, quite high. That is kind of nice, too, in its way. Dave had just given me a ball with the name of a lumber company and millworks on it, and that seemed especially apropos as it struck wood twice in two strokes. I hit another 5-wood, then another and another. Maybe that's what the numbers on the clubs mean: Hit the ball five times with the 5-wood.

My fifth shot on this hole goes into the water. Bert tosses me another ball, but the toss is short and it, too, goes into the water. It's that kind of day. I'm just thinking that all my shots are way too short, when someone else hits way too long, over the 13th green, and there is a loud THWACK! as the ball strikes the Bergen Community College Science Center. A good physics major in there can probably figure out how fast that ball was traveling when it impacted the building.

Bert tees off on 14 and again his drive hits just short of the green . . . on 16. He plays that shot into a sand trap on yet another hole before holing out with a 7. Playing on other fairways was fairly common. I experience a number of hockey-style face-offs on the 14th fairway with guys going in the opposite direction toward the 13th green. No shame in that. But you do have to hit the dirt occasionally when truly bad golfers are hitting balls right *at* you.

Billy—my partner!—is red hot, and dressed like he is, and with all his trash talk, he'd damned well better be. He's red hot and not at all gracious about it. I admire that: a guy who is doing really, really well and still takes the time to belittle those less fortunate. On Easter. On the par-3 15th, his drive lands three feet from the hole and he birdies it. On 16, I myself am "up and down," they tell me, meaning I chipped onto the green and 1-putted.

Again, the confidence is rising, the momentum's clearly on my side now, as I step to the next tee and drive what is to be the first of three attempts at a decent drive. After considering my options, I go with the second drive. I learn a valuable golf lesson. In golf, there is no frigging momentum.

I notice that over on an adjacent green, a guy is actually *throwing* his putter and yelling "goddamnedsonofabitch!" His companions look frightened. We critique his style, which is just a straight toss, rather than the preferred windmill whipping action you like to see.

Being guys, at the 18th tee we decide we'll all just hit the ball as hard as we can, and this approach always yields some breathtaking shots.

Let's talk about Dave's, shall we? Dave hits one of those drives that sort of reminds you of *Challenger*, as it rises majestically, higher and higher, farther and farther, like a rocket, and you go "ooooo"—*until* you begin to get this sick feeling in your stomach that something is going terribly wrong. In Dave's case, it's that his ball is going to land not one, but two fairways over. Bert gives him a lift in the cart, since he's going that way after his own drive anyway. Bert is just the one fairway to the right and his second shot carries over the correct fairway onto the fairway to the left just short of a cemetery. A friend of mine refers to this as "military golf: left-right-left-right."

Personally, I once again hit my ball into the sand, and while the three of them leave to retrieve their balls from fairways unknown, I take the opportunity to just pick up my damned ball and toss it. I haven't played in sand so much since kindergarten.

After I toss the ball, I kick it toward the hole for good measure. After the sand problem, I have somehow managed to hit two successive decent shots and am very excited to be putting to perhaps *win* the 18th hole outright, until I remember about the tossing and kicking.

I sink my putt, and joyously—because we're finished—toss the ball toward a Dodge Neon in the parking lot, but of course I miss that, too.

I am "in the clubhouse" with a solid 120. Bert holes out with an even 100. Dave a 91. Billy an 83. But, then, Billy has the scorecard. The team of Billy and me wins. My brother-in-law owes me six bucks (to this day). Once I get my 45 handicap legally established I'll be beating them all.

Being Easter and everything, I figure we'll all hustle home to our families. Nah. We go into the bar for breakfast. We are a group of mud-splattered heathens, taking our own sweet time before heading home to righteously ill tempered spouses, who have hunted colored eggs with the children, dressed them, and taken them to church on Easter morn.

We are golfers.

4

Do This, Don't Do That: A Game of Rules and Etiquette

Liz strongly suggested we learn the rules and etiquette of golf before hitting the course, and it was obvious I wouldn't be learning them from Bert, Billy, and Dave.

I purchased a copy of *The Rules of Golf* as approved by the United States Golf Association and the Royal and Ancient Golf Club of St. Andrews, Scotland, and was horrified. One hundred forty-four pages! And they said I really needed the companion 481-page *Decisions on the Rules of Golf* to boot.

It appeared that not only the USGA and all the Royals and Ancients had put their two cents in, but the Pope, the Supreme Court, and various and sundry state legislatures and city councils as well.

The books are as byzantine as any tort law tome I've ever laid eyes upon, chockablock with definitions and all manner of restrictions regarding provisional balls, casual water, crossing the margin, free drops, grounding of the club, lateral water hazards, loose impediments, nearest point of relief (not the men's room), and (ouch) embedded balls.

The rule book addresses such issues as whether snow and natural ice other than frost are "casual water" (any temporary accumulation of water on the course that is visible before or after the player takes his stance and is not in a water hazard) or "loose impediments" (natural objects such as stones, leaves, twigs, branches, and the like; dung, worms, insects, and casts or heaps made by them, provided they are not fixed or growing, are not solidly embedded, and do not adhere to the ball). Ice cubes, of course, are an "obstruction." Having determined whether said snow is "casual water" or a "loose impediment," the golfer must then turn to the applicable chapters to research what can legally be done about it. It's surprising that golfers are only accompanied by caddies, and not by golf attorneys as well.

Some sections are amusing, I must admit, and useful to players of my caliber, such as rule 25-3 regarding what to do when you find yourself on the "Wrong Putting Green."

The USGA receives hundreds of calls a year to rule on certain technicalities, and some of the decisions seem cruel. If your ball lands near an alligator in Orlando you must play it—dead or alive. A ball within ten feet of a rattlesnake in Arizona, however, may at times be deemed unplayable. If you hit a ball from within a water hazard and a fish is beached along with the ball and said fish blocks the next shot (not a common occurrence but it did happen in a recent NCAA women's championship), the fish may be tossed back in the water with no penalty—*if* it is still flopping. Alive, the fish is defined as an "outside agency"; dead, it's a "loose impediment" and moving it would cost you a stroke. Keep that in mind.

Keep *firmly* in mind that in 1974 the Ohio state legislature made cheating at golf a violation of the civil codes, and second-time offenders face up to a five-year prison term. Presumably, then, under the new three strikes law, the third time you mark yourself down for a 6 when you shot a 7 you'd get life, except in Texas where golfers would be made to play in lightning storms holding irons on their heads.

My attorneys advise me that all of these rules—no mulligans, no gimmees, no throwies, no kickies, no adjustable scoring practices—make shooting a decent score next to impossible for law-abiding golfers and they strongly suggest I do my golfing outside Ohio.

If rules are what you can't do, etiquette is what you shouldn't do. So many don'ts in golf. Hundreds of books out there on golf etiquette. Other sports have rules, but I'm not sure any others even *have* etiquette. Show me the etiquette primer for the National Hockey League.

Mr. Golf Etiquette's Golf Etiquette Primer talks of manners and courtesy, suggesting we be quiet and not run on the golf course, and when we walk "walk quickly but lightly." No, golf is not at all like other sports.

There's to be no laughing or talking at the tees. Moreover you're not to even so much as *move* while others are teeing off. Have they thought of having a nun with a ruler there to rap offenders' knuckles? Shouldn't golf at least be a little more like recess?

Like the rules of golf, some golf etiquette seems ridiculously complex. You practically need a state license (written and practical exams) to tend the flag stick, for example. When putting, your ball may not strike the flag stick (2-stroke penalty), so a fellow golfer must hold it while you putt and remove it while your putt is on its way. The laws of etiquette demand that when tending the flag stick, you must stand to the left or right of the cup, ensuring that your shadow does not fall on the hole or on the ball's path. You are to stand an arm's length from the hole, taking care not to stand on the path other players' putts will have to travel so as not to indent said paths. You are to hold the flag itself against the flag stick so as not to allow it to flap in the wind. You are to "become invisible," not fidgeting or talking. You lift the stick after the putt is stroked and lay it down in a prescribed manner (we'll not even get into that here) off the green. You are not to ever, *ever* forget to replace the flag stick.

Recently I tended a flag stick at an exclusive private club. I'm quite sure I did it wrongly, but the other golfers were polite enough not to mention it. I yanked out the flag stick as the long, difficult putt rolled directly toward the hole. However, not only the stick, but the entire hole—about an eight-inch-long steel cylinder—came out of the ground and the ball clanked against its side. These things just have a way of happening to me on a golf course.

Liz was big on etiquette. She said other golfers don't really mind how bad you are, only how rude and inconsiderate (to include slow). If I understand her correctly, if you say, "Please excuse me for hitting that drive into the club dining room and placing your mother in a coma," you're fine. "It was my fervent hope that it would sink rather than skip when it struck her bowl of soup."

On the tee, Liz suggests: "Wait until the group in front of you has completed their second shot." Otherwise they get PO'd when your ball lands amongst them. (When you're bad, you never know how far your ball is going to go.) She said players have been known to purposely hit a shot into the group ahead to send them a message they're playing too slowly. Be aware, however, that groups hit into have been known to retaliate by teeing up a ball and hitting it back at the menacing group behind them. This is most un-genteel and completely out of place, a form of guerrilla golf not to be condoned.

"Keep it moving," she says. "Slow golf is the biggest complaint in the sport. Know who has honors [who won the last hole and tees off first]." Hint: It's not you!

5

Driving Ourselves to Drink

I am not at home on the range. Not in the least. I am as out of place and potentially dangerous on the driving range as I am on the course itself.

It was suggested by my Easter partners that I practice and hone my skills at the driving range—"golf's laboratory"—before hitting the links again. It's a weekday in May, before the summer rush, so there shouldn't be too many people around. A good day for a couple of bad golfers like my son Willie and myself to hit the range.

We select our clubs from two bags in the garage. One bag belonged to a late stepfather-in-law and contains a few nasty clubs left over after a brother-in-law took the ones he wanted. The other bag is a set I purchased (Wal-Mart?) on sale for my son that should have carried a warning label stating "Caution: Too Short For People" and are way too short for tall people like him. Also, they are not your top-o'-the-line clubs. I forget the brand.

53

Popeil, I believe. He's brought them home with him from his apartment not to play golf, but with the intention of leaving them here. They apparently wouldn't fit in the Goodwill bin and anyway statistics show that really poor people don't play golf. Although they should. They might be more successful. Ever notice how many golfers are also successful in business? Why, poor people might even become *doctors* if they played enough golf.

We're headed to a run-of-the-mill driving range on a run-of-the-mill public course for run-of-the-mill golfers—although we personally haven't achieved that level yet. The bartender sells us two five-dollar tokens for the golf ball machine, and points us in the direction of the driving range, which is a long way down a steep incline on a winding lane—a good safe distance from the clubhouse.

A feeling of exhilaration comes over us as the tees, the empty tees, come into view. No one is there, and it's secluded. No one will see us here in the woods. We don't like people to watch.

The golf ball machine issues us forty balls each in two cute little wire baskets. Someday such machines will be able to read our retinas, identify us as nuisance golfers, and refuse to issue us golf balls without a license. When you're as bad as we are, there should probably be a three-day waiting period.

We tee up our first balls of the day. Willie hits his first, a little chopper that would be a foul ball in baseball, to the left of third base, and just about that far. His second, third, and fourth drives are pretty much the same, but the fifth is an improvement, a grounder where the shortstop would be. Such shots are bad golf shots, of course, but not all bad here on a driving range, as they remain so close at hand that they can be retrieved and hit again—at a savings of 12.5 cents each.

Pros tell us in their little instruction booklets that golfers really only hit one fourth of the ball. Willie has chosen to hit the *top* quartile. As mentioned, he is tall and his clubs woefully short. I tell him to stoop down, although I don't believe I've ever heard a golf instructor specifically say "stoop down," not per se. He doesn't listen to my advice, nor should he.

Sometimes he swings so high that he whiffs, missing the ball altogether. When I hear the Whoosh! of a good miss like that, I always look over to see Willie fighting back a laugh, or sometimes a curse, but always pretending it has been a practice swing. "Okay, let's get started," he'll say.

I don't hit the ball on top. I hit it low, on the bottom, sometimes very low, sometimes striking the mat behind the ball rather than the ball itself. Hitting the ball like this makes it go very high, sometimes so high you can't see it when you look downrange, until it plops down about fifty yards away. This shot is known in some quarters as an "Elephant's Ass," because it is high and it stinks.

Sometimes the shot only goes twenty-five yards. I think this is because of the backspin that some golfers spend years trying to achieve but which comes to me quite naturally. You see it on TV, where a professional's shot will land, "bite" the green, and roll backward nearer the hole. Mine never do that on the greens, however, just on the tee shots.

I have been to covered driving ranges, where they put a

little roof over the golfers' heads for protection from in-clement weather. Although these roofs are quite high and project out only a couple of feet in front of the tee, I can, and do, hit these roofs when my drives go straight up. Usually, driving range tees also have short little wooden protective walls separating them, walls that project only a foot or two in front of the tees, and I can, and have, hit those as well with drives traveling sideways at almost 90 degree angles.

My first drive this day at the range is high, as usual, but not too high, and pretty straight . . . for about fifty yards . . . where it encounters some strange force, possibly isolated wind shear, that makes the ball peel off to the right in a beautiful curve, really, that carries it toward the high netting meant to protect surrounding flora and fauna from the likes of me.

My son handles the play-by-play à la Mets announcer Bob Murphy calling a Mike Piazza home run: "This ball is high, it is deep, it is going, going, gone, goodbye, this ball is outta here, folks!"

The drive has carried over the protective netting and landed in the woods. If Mark McGwire hit that every-body would be cheering. Tiger Woods, too. Pro golfers hit shots like that all the time, hooks and slices that are called "fade" and "draw" shots, which they hit purposely to go around trees. So shut up.

Drives like this tell me I must somehow be hitting the bottom *and* the side of the ball at the same time—two quarters at once! No mean feat. That was the first of many of my shots to clear the netting this day. I came to appre-ciate the wide range of percussive sounds the balls made when they hit the trees, discriminating amongst those that cracked and crashed against limbs, thunked richly against trunks, made muffled sounds as they struck way back in the woods, and the rare double or even triple thwacks of a ball ricocheting through the woodlands on this lovely spring day. It made you wish Robert Frost had been a bad golfer: "The woods are lovely dark and deep, shanks and slices yon forests keep . . ."

Willie grows frustrated. If all the drives he hit were bad, it would honestly be better. But this evil enterprise gives one a fleeting glimpse of solid improvement, then snatches it away. He hits some straight, long beauties, and feels he's finally really getting this game, then follows them with a half dozen horrors.

It is at this point that he slowly and gracefully takes a few steps forward and, maintaining complete control, ever so gently tosses his club just ten yards downrange.

I return to the same driving range with my wife, Jody, whose golf skills are well matched to those of other members of the family.

Forty golf balls tumble into my basket and it occurs to me that this is just what I need when I play real golf: a basket of balls. Or perhaps a golf ball machine towed behind my cart.

This time, we are not alone on the range. There are three young boys, about nineteen or twenty years old I'd say, dressed in T-shirts, shorts, and sandals. I hope they won't be good. They don't disappoint me.

They swing hard like baseball players, and like baseball players they miss the ball a lot. (So, why is it called a strike, when one fails to strike the ball?) Their drives are highly erratic, traveling somewhere in the one- to two-hundred-yard range.

My favorite technique of theirs is one in which they stand back ten feet, then charge the ball and swing at it wildly. They see this as a way of generating immense power, but it doesn't seem to work. They're swinging so hard that after a while they complain that their backs hurt. So, what does work?

"I took off my shoes and that seemed to help," says one.

Focus seems to help. A target. A deer wanders out on the course, about 250 yards downrange, and the boys suddenly get a lot better. They hit the ball farther and with more accuracy as they try to hit the deer. Now, understand—People for the Ethical Treatment of Animals—that deer are not beloved here, where there are more of them than there are of us, where they dispense lyme disease, cause traffic fatalities, and devour our shrubs and flower beds. Understand, too, that these boys don't stand a chance in hell of hitting the deer. It might make for an interesting sport though, come to think of it, combining a driving range with a game farm, where you'd get 100 points for hitting a deer at 200 yards, maybe 50 for a prairie dog at 100 yards, 5 for an elephant at 50 yards— that sort of thing. Understand, furthermore, that this idea comes from someone who wanted to liven up the Winter Olympics by having biathlon (skiing and shooting) competitors fire at speed skaters as they went by a hole in a fence.

We run out of balls at the same time the boys do. We all look at each other, look up the hill to see if anyone is watching, then the five of us dart out onto the range and as fast as we can pick up dozens and dozens of balls lying within twenty-five yards or so of the tees, then dart back to the tees again.

Now, you need not practice at a driving range. I've seen a guy practicing his bunker shots in the sand box at a local elementary school.

You can practice golf almost anywhere, even in your own backyard. Indeed, lots of golf nuts are installing regulation putting greens in their backyards.

I practice putting in the house, using an electric putting hole gadget my son gave me that spits the balls back. My cats love to chase my putts and bat them about, and frankly are as good at getting them in the hole as I am. I'm getting better as I learn to read the break on the hardwood floors in our 107-year-old house.

On vacations, we hold chipping and driving contests in the yard. We try to chip balls about fifty feet into swimming pool tubes we've scattered about. Our friend Pam won the contest and the six-pack by chipping one into a bucket! Magnificent shot. At some point we take aim at the swimming pool itself, although this always results in a certain amount of collateral damage to the house, the wooden fence, the garden, and the patio furniture—in part, because we're drunk. I am quite good at chipping balls into the pool; hitting balls into water just seems to come naturally to me.

We also hit drives toward the bay, endangering beachgoers, protected wetlands, egrets, and neighboring homes. It also ruins the lawn as we take toupee-sized divots out of the yard. The inlet and marsh is only about 150 yards out, so a golf ball splashdown is good, but a shot onto the beach (some 200 to 250 yards away) that hits an umbrella or scatters sunbathers is excellent. For this we use the five-for-a-dollar "previously owned" balls from a stand next to the local course. Around Easter every year we have a used golf ball hunt in the thorny thickets extending from the edge of our yard to the inlet.

After Jody receives a nice set of clubs for her birthday (even though she's never played) we decide to inaugurate them at another driving range on a cool spring day. This is right after Liz's golf class and I'm most eager to find out just how much my game's improved.

Easier said than done here in golf-crazed suburbia. But as dusk settles, spaces do finally begin to open up. I see another novice put a token into the ball machine, fail to place the basket directly under the spout, and the cascading golf balls roll everywhere. I am secretly pleased, beginning to think that maybe for once I won't look like the fool of the day.

There is no privacy. But to my great joy I don't seem to need it so much anymore. The lessons seem to have helped. My 7- and 9-iron shots are going straighter, some even landing on the greens at fifty and a hundred yards! Of course they roll off the greens, in shots that TV commentators would lament, and true there are no sand traps here, but for me this is spectacular. And, I seem to be hitting fewer off the sideboards. Thank you, Liz.

My driving, however, remains as poor as ever. My irons are going straighter and just as far as my driver shots. My drives are short—even with a titanium driver!—and thickly sliced. And, I still can't hit the damned guy in the ball retrieval cart (there is no People for the Ethical Treatment of People). Once the ball retrieval cart went by just five feet in front of my tee and it was tempting, believe me.

There is a certain amount of chuckling coming from observers on benches behind us, but I choose to believe they are watching their awful friend next to me. It's the guy who spilled the balls, and who is now hitting some of them as little as three feet off the tee. Dribblers. And God bless him.

6

Golf Wars Weaponry

Maybe it's my socks.

"Could very well be," suggested the helpful sales-man . . . of socks. Maybe it is. Maybe my golf game sucks because of bad socks.

As Americans, we have a deep and abiding faith in, tend to place all of our hopes and dreams for the future in . . . technology. We the people do further believe that stuff we buy will make our lives better and happier. And although golfers are among the best educated of any sportsmen and -women, they have this weakness, this ad-diction, that leaves them completely vulnerable to dealers of anything—anything!—that claims to take one single, solitary stroke off their scores.

Which brings us, Jody and me, to a veritable Mecca of golf technology and other assorted claptrap: the PGA Golf Merchandise Show in Orlando, Florida, to see what sort of breakthroughs the scientific community—physicists and engineers!—has made to ease the pain of struggling duffers like ourselves.

This show—this lalapalooza of golf technology—is enough to make one wonder how any golfer could *possibly* be bad! Here before us, spreading way beyond the indoor horizon, are *sixteen hundred* booths purveying humongous zirconium-titanium drivers, possum-skin gloves, computer swing analyzers, laser putters, Hole-In-One nutrition bars, neodymium and polybutadiene core balls, golf global positioning systems—you name it—each and every advanced product claiming to take strokes off our games.

We spend two full days walking up and down the aisles, each step potentially lowering our golf scores, and each step adding to our bedazzlement at the overwhelming resources brought to bear on this national priority: getting a ball in a hole.

"To play golf well, you need good socks. It's as simple as that." That is the considered opinion of the foot covering expert at the Winning Greens & Fairways Performance Socks booth, a man who's spent his whole life in socks. Not just any socks, golf socks—*performance* golf socks. Crew, anklet, or lo-cut.

Now, how, exactly, will these socks *perform* for me? He explains how the special ribbing increases circulation: "It's one-by-one stitching. Doesn't pinch the foot. The feet don't get tired."

How many strokes is a good pair of golf socks worth?

"Well," he answers, "that varies with the individual, of

course, but obviously if you have bad socks, your game suffers." Obviously. "On the back 9 your dogs start barkin', you start thinking about your feet, and there you go. It's a mental game and your feet can become very mental."

Mental feet. Umm-hmm. So . . . how many strokes?

"A couple of strokes."

Performance Golf Socks: –2 strokes

Next booth. Shoes.

"If you think good socks can help your game, imagine what proper footwear will do," says the shoe rep. "Our Cyclonic spikelets golf shoes with premolded rubber bottoms provide a 25 percent larger platform with strategically placed cleats and treads to increase traction and stability."

Also at the show are new golf sandals, which I'm sure violate most country club dress codes, especially those highly provocative open-toed models. Not for me. I have these new socks and only guys from Bulgaria and Boulder wear socks with sandals.

Staid, old Florsheim offers "biomagnetic" shoes. Another company sells every conceivable style and color of alligator golf shoes, to include alligator cowboy golf boots. Just how big is golf these days? Well, they claim to have thirty thousand gators on their farm just dying to become golf shoes. Thirty thousand! Little wonder that every once in a while a vindictive gator takes revenge and eats a Florida golfer. But: What is lost?

How many strokes will good golf shoes take off my score?

"A few" is the consensus.

Better Shoes: –3 strokes

Not to mention cleats, which may seem like a small thing, but are not. (For want of a nail the shoe was lost, for want of a shoe the horse was lost, for want of a horse the battle was lost, etc.)

"Cleats can be critical," proclaims the Eagle Grip soft cleats salesman, and the Softspikes representative agrees: "Our Black Widow model is the new standard, offering unparalleled traction, anti-clogging, and is available in four installation systems: small thread, large thread, the new Champ-Q-Lok, fast twist. They can make an enormous difference."

Proper Cleats: –1 stroke (we think "enormous" is hyperbolic)

"You know your problem?" shouts the barker, literally grabbing us as we walk by. "You don't have dry hands! It's ruining your game!"

Lucky for me, he has Dry Hands lotion, "the ultimate gripping solution!," which he is now frantically squirting on my palms even though I didn't ask him to. "It actually repels water and perspiration! Hit those hands with some water!" he blurts at his assistant, who immediately pours a glass of water on my palms—and the water rolls right off!

I have very dry, very milky-colored hands for the rest of the day.

Dry Hands: -2 strokes, he says: "At least!"

Tees! Do you mean to tell me it actually matters what kind of *tees* I use?

"Absolutely!" barks the tee man. "Our tees employ advanced technological advances."

Okay, then. His Perfect-Tee, for example, has not one prong but two! How's *that* for progress? It has two prongs for greater distance, "more confidence," consistent ball height, and adjustable ball trajectory.

I tell him that I already have adjustable ball trajectory. Mine adjusts, automatically, without any input from me, from wormburner to the bottle rocket trajectory. But before you go getting cynical on me, just listen to this Perfect-Tee endorsement from James C. White of Birmingham, Alabama: "I had no trouble with my balls falling off in high winds." Nobody wants that.

Direct-A-Tee is a bent, 45 degree angle tee, for—guess what? More distance and accuracy through "scientific development." And! It is the golf tee of the future. Another tee boasts its "biodegradability," which means it's wood. Also, "it goes in the ground easier"—and you know how tired you get pushing those damned tees in the ground all day, especially when you use tees for almost every shot (except putting), like I do.

Also, there's a "South African revolutionary" tee. We didn't even know South African revolutionaries were golfers. We figured it was the white guys. With this one, you set the ball on toothbrush bristles, the Brush-T. "Wood and plastic," said a rather unrevolutionary-looking sales rep, "are over."

"How many strokes will it take off my game?"

"On average? Three or more."

Techno Tees: –3 strokes

Perhaps the greatest advance at the show, although Jody may beg to differ, is embodied in two attractive young women advancing toward us, passing out literature for their services. No one brushes aside *their* brochures and *everybody* reads them, carefully.

They're the product, offered by Caddy Girls USA, a firm (very) providing comely, young—but legal—women in short skirts to caddie for you, the golfer. The picture on the brochure shows just such a babe going over a (golf) scorecard with a client as they sit together, very snugly, in a cart. The brochure reads: "Need a caddy? Have more fun. From the bag drop until the final putt on the 18th green Caddy Girls will caddy, encourage, and entertain the entire round. Caddy Girls offers a team of attractive, knowledgeable, and entertaining girls that will make any golf outing a memorable event."

It stays away from terms like "scoring" and "strokes," but "encourage," "entertain," "bag drop"—it all sounds beneficial to my game.

Caddy Girls: +5 strokes

Carts are, of course, critical. I actually own my own. It came with a house we bought, thrown in by the sellers for two hundred bucks. Right away it needed $300 worth of batteries, a new tire, and several other repairs. It has yet to be on a golf course. My nieces and nephews love it, driving it ceaselessly around and around the yard, killing the grass and nearly themselves, while screaming at each other all day over whose turn it is to drive. The guys at the local auto repair shop love my golf cart, which is kind of an annuity for them—a golden goose that just keeps on giving. The shop has done about $1,000 in repairs to it over the last three years. The kids drove it into the bushes and hung it up on a tree stump, destroying the steering. They ruined the ignition system. They crashed it into and through our fence. Finally, they hit the house itself, causing $800 in damage. One time, our nieces and nephews didn't break it—my daughter's teenaged friends did. They took it out for a spin (possibly after a few beers) on some rural roads, a venture on which they were spotted (despite having camouflaged it with weeds and tree branches) driving it into the local airport and onto a ferry boat. They returned pushing the broken cart, which bore a cargo of stolen lawn ornaments. You wouldn't think there'd be all that many things that could go wrong with a simple golf cart, but there are, especially when it's used as an all-terrain vehicle.

There are fancy carts at the show costing almost as much as cars. Some look like street hot rods—'35 Chevies and '34 Fords—outfitted with coolers under the hoods, phone jacks, brake lights, horns, cigarette lighters, and turn signals. There are classy Duesenberg estate golf carts, too.

And you know those pull carts? For about $1,100 you don't have to pull them. You push buttons on a remote control and the TS-1 Lectronic Kaddy runs all over the course, terrifying other golfers. "You'll want the 'Hill Tamer' feature," says the salesman. Hell yes. Got to have Hill Tamer. And "worm gear drive"! Sure. The company motto is "Break par, not your back."

If you don't want to spend that kind of dough, there's the Cart Wizard, which Velcros the pull cart to the back of your belt and you pull it like a horse pulling a cart.

"You can't underestimate the fatigue factor in golf," says the salesman. "It could cost you five strokes, minimum."

Golf Cart: -5 strokes (although the pros walk, and Warning: Golf carts with built-in beer coolers may double your score on the back 9)

I play bare-handed and that is wrong. Golf gloves make all the difference. For one thing you look cooler, and you have a better grip (especially when you or your beer can is sweating). "Steve" says he wears his when he's masturbating. That way he doesn't give himself any sexually transmittable diseases.

If you give a tinker's damn about our rain forests you'll buy possum-skin gloves. Personally, it makes *my* skin crawl to think of touching that of a possum, but it turns out the little bastards are destroying New Zealand's rain forests! Read the brochure for the Gripper natural possum-skin gloves: "Brought to New Zealand in 1837, the possum flourished in the absence of natural predators and now poses a serious environmental threat to New Zealand's native rain forest, consuming 21,000 tons of foliage per day!!! By attempting to keep the possum population in check, the Gripper is helping to preserve and maintain New Zealand's delicate balance of nature."

Kill 'Em and Wear 'Em. Now!

I don't know if the kangaroo is destroying Australia's rain forests or not, or if Australia even has any rain forests, but you can help by buying K'Rooz kangaroo leather golf gloves, which are thinner yet last four times longer than cabretta leather, according to a usually reliable source, the Kangaroo Industry Association of Australia. "You'll feel more confidence and have lower scores," they say.

There are fleece-lined gloves for nuts who play in cold weather, gloves with magnets and copper inserts, special cart driving gloves, and the Crazy Q glove, which has weights in it and may actually allow you to cheat undetected. Like illegally weighted bats in baseball, these weighted gloves are said to increase impact power by 5 to 10 percent, causing ten to twenty yards of extra distance.

Possum, Kangaroo, or Cheating Gloves: –3 strokes

One of my favorite products at the show is "GOLF—the essence of the game" cologne, "crisp and clean with a sophistication associated with low handicappers." Maybe if I just wear this! Maybe it's like aromatherapy. "You keep thinking golf long after leaving the course" when you wear this fragrance made with "extract of fairway grass" clippings. It has "grassy overtones . . . smells like the golf course."

Will it actually take strokes off my game?

"Spray it on your balls and it might surprise you!" is the snappy retort.

Golf Cologne: –1 stroke

"To be competitive, you'll need the modern tools of the trade," says the guy in the next booth, when I tell him I'm taking up the game. "It's almost to where you can't play without this little honey." Little honey is the Bushnell Yardage Pro Rangefinder, which looks like a pair of binoculars. You point it at the flag—or the beverage cart—and it gives you the distance. "Personally," I tell him, "I'd really rather not be reminded." Not to mention I usually can't see the damned flag for all the trees.

There are all sorts of divot repair tools, one of them gold. Why? "Status," says the salesman. "Weird," we reply. The little gadgets would do me no good. Most of my divots require earthmoving equipment to replace.

There's the Deluxe Golf Pro Swiss Army knife, which could come in handy when you hit into the very, very rough and need survival tools and skills. This special model has the club groove cleaner, spike wrench, snap shackle, divot repair tool, cigar cutter, Phillips head screwdriver, bottle cap lifter, can opener, toothpick, and tweezers. "Or," I suggest, "if your game's going really badly, you could use the knife to slit your wrists."

"Absolutely," says the agreeable salesman.

There is one tool I really can use: JTD's Search 'N Rescue line of golf ball retrieval units, for recovering balls hit into the water. There are one-, two-, and even four-ball retrievers—in case you're playing in a really bad foursome or you've personally hit four consecutive tries into the water. The salesman says his father started the business twenty years ago in the (presumably wet) basement. What will he do for a living if someone invents a floating golf ball? "Still need to retrieve the little sucker," he smiles. He does have stiff competition, however, from the likes of the Mud Weasel, which can also retrieve four balls at a time up to fifteen feet away using an anodized aluminum shaft that cannot rust or corrode.

We see a guy walking around with a car antenna he says is the Finders Keepers golf ball detector. He looks like a product of the patients' rights movement that emptied so many of our fine mental institutions. He puts a ball on the floor and when he walks past it, the antenna points at the ball. Which is fine, except that when I walk past the ball holding the antenna, it does not point at the ball. "You're not doing it right," he advises. Why hasn't anyone ever come out with a Lo-Jack golf ball?

And there is a global positioning system device for golfers called the inFOREmer 2000. Jesus, do some people get *that* far out in the rough? The handheld electronic appliance displays the hole you're on, distance to the pin and hazards, distance to the front and the back of the green, professional tips for playing the hole, a weather advisory, digital scoring, green contours and undulations, the distance of each shot, and it retrieves messages and memos, as well as issuing 911 emergency calls. The most appealing capability was the suggestion that it could possibly be used for calling in food and beverage orders.

Tools of the Trade: –3 strokes

Industro-Weld paste has a booth. "Why?" I ask. "So if you throw your clubs and the heads fall off you can glue 'em back on?"

"Exactly."

Club Repair Paste: –3 strokes (it could mean a couple hundred strokes if you had to play with your clubheads off)

You can lose your head and you can also lose the whole club. "Can't play with lost clubs now, canya?" Nosir.

The salesman says ClubOut prevents club loss. It's a bunch of tubes you place your clubs in and when you remove them a red gizmo pops up to alert you that the club is out and probably still lying next to the green where you left it, stupid.

Can't play with your clubs *stolen* either, now, canya? More than 800,000 golf clubs worth about $100 million were stolen last year—so maybe golfers are not a nicer class of people after all, eh? Either that or the good folks at the Club Alert booth are trying to scare us. They insert a transmitter into each club, which emits a light and sound alert when the club and bag are separated by more than sixty feet.

It remains to be seen if this new product will become as thoroughly obnoxious and universally despised as car alarms, but here in this last bastion of serenity, the golf course, it certainly has a decent chance.

Club Alarms: +1 stroke

There's an almost infinite variety of training aids on display here, most of them really odd-looking contraptions you strap to your body to remind you that you're doing many things horribly wrong. Would that you could wear all these while you play! You'd look like a B-movie Martian but you'd never make a mistake.

The Alignment Plus looks like a car antenna that you

strap horizontally across your chest—undoubtedly causing immense pain and suffering to women golfers—but: aligning feet and body; promoting "proper take-away" and shoulder turn; keeping you "parallel" to your target; and improving your "alignment."

There are golf training devices you strap to your legs, arms, and wrists. There's the muscle memory Pivot-maker board you strap to your feet like a snowboard; the Mad Jack Swing Machine training system, a huge tubular contraption that's a "slice breaker/swing builder" and may or may not fit in the house; and the Kneeknocker, which "uses the proven biofeedback technique" to train you to keep the right knee flexed during the backswing. That is: If your knee straightens, the sensor beeps.

There are lots of items employing big rubber bands— aka "golf tension bands"—offering muscle building through resistance for greater clubhead speed. And there is a Swingometer and the Excel-A-Rater to measure it.

And there's a kinky bondage variety that appears to be borrowed from the S&M industry or from restraints used in the transport of dangerous prisoners. One of these straps your arms together to restrict arm separation, another one straps your legs together to inhibit lateral sway, and then there are, well, handcuffs that remind you to keep your hands together.

All this to turn you into the perfect golf machine.

Training Devices: –15 combined strokes

It is unclear to me if the Perfect Grip is a training device or something you can permanently attach to the top of your club shaft. It is pro golfer Mark O'Meara's grip, something that looks as though the golfer had gripped a wad of clay, then had it molded in plastic. You just put your hands where his were and presumably play just like him.

Also, there is offered at the show a bronze sculpture of Moe (not Greg) Norman's golf grip—his two hands gripping the top of a golf club—for study and reflection and to beautify any home. We put our hands behind our backs and admired it. To a golfer, a thing of beauty, one would guess, provided of course that Moe Norman is or was a golfer. We just don't know.

Getting a Grip: –3 strokes

There is a disturbing amount of emphasis at the show on pain relief. Most of it focuses on physical pain, however, when clearly what is needed is help with the emotional and psychological varieties.

The emphasis ranges from Advil, here to tout its sponsorship of the senior tour, to perhaps twenty booths offering copper or magnetic wristbands that claim to cure arthritis and (most) other maladies.

"The Tour Power copper-magnetic wristbands provide copper to your body and allow more oxygen-rich blood to flow to your muscles," explains the pitchman. "Biomagnetism works in the human body through the circulatory system, the nervous system, and the endocrine system to take strokes off your game."

There are magnetic gloves and gel insoles, acupuncture insoles, ionized yin-yang bracelets that are "a Gift of God," and whole wearable electromagnetic fields by PulseGen.

On display is the HP-568 Lux I massage chair for golfers, which did feel damned good after two days of walking the merchandise show. And the Golf-Doc first aid kit, with big bandages in it! Not since my friend was smacked by a windmill blade on the miniature golf course have I seen a need for bandages on a golf course.

Out in the hallway, where booth space is cheaper, there is a man hanging—all day long—by both arms from what appears to be a swing set or medieval torture device. He is smiling, however, because he wants others to think he is enjoying himself and to buy his Soft Stretch machine that stretches out golfers in just the right way and makes them feel better.

Pain Relief (physical): -3 strokes

Cosmetology comes into play. You need sun protection, of course, but not just any sun protection, special sun protection formulated especially for golfers, like "Claro skincare especially for golfers" that is nongreasy and sweatproof. When golf clubs fly out of your hands, it should be on purpose, in anger.

Titanium is a magic word in the golf kingdom these

days and there's even a titanium golfer's sunblock called Golfstik. I wonder if you look like the Tin Man after application.

"If you don't think sun protection will improve your game, just try playing with a really bad sunburn sometime, buster," says Valerie from behind the Claro counter.

Golf Sunscreen: -3 strokes

"If you look good, you play good," says the golf clothing salesman. "It goes without saying. It's all about confidence."

The days of those hideous pink and green plaid golf pants for men are, unfortunately, over. It's the one aspect of the game I truly enjoyed.

Today's golfer looks like Al Gore running for President, after consultants told him he looked too Washingtonian and he began wearing casual earth-toned polo shirts (Excuse me, is that the new Polo goose crap green you're wearing?). When Gore wears them, they too look dull, by association. Like dress-down Fridays at the funeral home.

So these guys tell me I must spend scads of money on top-of-the-line, drab golf wear. But should I? Is there anything worse than looking like a pro and playing like . . . me? And where to begin? All pro golfers seem to have their own lines on display at the show: Ben Crenshaw, Greg Norman, Jack Nicklaus, the noted golfer Tommy Hilfiger, Leon Levin (should I know him or is he Tiger Woods's CPA?), Fuzzy Zoeller. Bobby Jones has a line but I don't want to look like him . . . dead. There is also a line of nice golf clothes called Divots for some reason, which might be just the thing for me.

Sharp (i.e., Dull) Clothes: -1 stroke

"The hat you wear *will* make a difference in your golf game," suggests the Tilley Hat salesman.

While the new Miracle Visor at the show is "headache free," "windproof," and "dishwasher safe," and the Greg Norman and Crocodile Dundee hats are enticing, we like best the extraordinary sales pitch for the Tilley Hat. It's worn, we're told, by elephant trainer Michael Hackenberger, of the Bowmanville Zoo in Ontario, who has had his Tilley eaten and thoroughly digested by an elephant three times. He has retrieved it, back there in the back, each time and still wears it. "That ought to tell you something!" says the enthusiastic pitchman. Like: never stand downwind from Michael Hackenberger.

Hat: -1 stroke

We didn't see any golf *pills* at the show, something I had seen at an infomercial convention in Vegas. Yes, there was a claim that taking a pill made you a better golfer. However, we did find at the PGA show Hole-In-One-Bars, snack treats sporting three power-packed herbs: ginseng, ginkgo, and guarana—the ginseng presumably for more energy to drive the ball; the ginkgo perhaps to give you the mental acuity to cheat wisely; and the guarana to . . . uh . . . replenish the body's crying need for guarana after golfing? The bars come in lemon crisp, banana zinger, chocolate crunch, and the new peanut butter chocolate, and are also available in baseball, basketball, football, soccer, and tennis wrappers.

Will this bar make me hit a hole-in-one? And can I eat eighteen in one day? "We cannot totally guarantee immediate holes-in-ones, but it should improve your game," says the sales rep.

Wash it down with Gatorade, according to folks at that booth, and your scores will plummet. Not to mention what will happen if you drop in a couple of LiFizz effervescent vitamin tablets, official vitamins of the PGA Tour.

There is even a booth pushing human growth hormone spray, or "biogevity" spray, for better golf, not to mention enhanced "athletic performance, energy, cardiovascular functions, cholesterol levels, sexual function, musculature, weight management, injury/surgery healing, and feelings and vigor of youth." The mouth spray is touted as cheaper and less painful than human growth hormone injections and can be carried in your pocket or golf bag. More socially acceptable than shooting up on the first tee, too.

There are special golfers' chocolates and golfers' peanuts that have unspecified benefits. Maybe they're titanium peanuts.

Hole-In-One-Bars washed down with Gatorade spiked

with official PGA Tour vitamins and a spritz of human growth hormone: –5 strokes

And finally there is the power of prayer. At the Fellowship of Christian Athletes Golf Ministry ("impacting the world for Christ through golf") booth, a representative reminds us that God is all powerful and could definitely help our golf games if He or She so chooses.

But there are famines, wars, pestilence, floods, and so forth that could distract Him or Her from lending a hand with our putting. And we reminded ourselves that He or She just might decide to adversely affect our games, too, especially when we're playing on Sunday mornings when we're supposed to be worshiping Him or Her.

God: –2 strokes (tough to figure, but we think the Omnipotent One oughta be good for 2 strokes—providing we don't yell "Goddamnit!" or "Why God, Why?" after every shank, hook, slice, sand trap, or flubbed putt, for chrissake)

So, let's see, that works out to a grand total of:

–59 strokes (if you forgo the Caddy Girls and club alarms). And we still haven't deducted a massive number of strokes for space age golf clubs and high-tech balls.

I still won't break 80, but it's a start . . . on one man's journey to a glimmer of respectability.

7

Tiger and Me: Different Strokes for Different Folks

Maybe if I watch Tiger Woods on TV, and imitate him. Golfers do, you know. I've seen them watching golf on TV and swinging their clubs along with him right there in the family room. Just like their wives do to Richard Simmons's *Sweatin' to the Oldies* tapes. The golfers break stuff, sometimes, lamps and things, but it's for a good cause.

It's a perfect summer Sunday, 80 degrees, sunny and dry with just a wisp of a breeze. I know that only by way of the Weather Channel, because I'm sitting indoors all afternoon watching golf on television as are 20 million other Americans. Have we no *lives?*

The telecast is sponsored by the good (solid) people at Viagra, which is a complete waste of money unless they can make the pitch to all these golf zombies that they might be able to use their new erections for putting. Their wives would have to dress up in Astroturf and lie down like a green to get any action from this crowd. And even then, I wouldn't bet on it, wouldn't take the flag stick out.

Tiger Woods is on! He's battling at Valhalla in Louisville for the PGA Championship, which he won the year before, and will of course win this time as everybody watching already knows. It's worse than the World Wrestling Federation, where the underdog occasionally wins to maintain the suspense. Not here, not in professional golf, not since Tiger arrived.

I grab one of my wife's irons and watch. But Tiger's game is difficult to relate to. These touring professionals aren't really playing the same game as you and I. Their shots look a lot different and there seem to be far fewer of them. And where are the mulligans? The gimmees? How can they *play* like this?

Their shots even sound different, neat little Clicks! Not like mine that go: Thdth! Nwack! Thwup! Boink! Blutz! Gank! and Frang!

Once in a while I hit a shot like the pros hit, and once in a while they hit a shot like I do. But you really have to look closely for their negatives to find common ground.

And, yes, between those three-hundred-yard drives and thirty-foot putts, the negatives *are* there—even for Tiger. I watch him and am pleasantly surprised to note that he is clearly upset about his golf game much of the time— just like me! He shakes his head and mutters to himself when his shots don't turn out the way he'd hoped. Just like me. Except, of course, his hopes are somewhat higher.

I see Tiger seething when he misses a twenty-five-foot putt—same as me, except mine would be three feet. His putt is for 2 under, mine for somewhere over. He sticks his tongue out at the ball. I stick out my finger.

Later, this very best golfer in the world actually misses a one-and-one-half-foot putt! For a double-bogey! I understand. I've had rounds with double-bogeys, too, but I was happy about them.

He hits one into a little creek and the announcer explains he was "too quick in his transition." I start to write that down, but realize he might just as well have said "transmission" because I don't know what the hell he's talking about.

Tiger also puts his ball in a sand trap. Now, this is where I'd discreetly toss it at the hole. But he really can't. Big gallery, big TV audience. And, anyway, his blast out of the sand lands *6 inches* from the hole—and, frankly, I can't throw it that accurately.

And I *loved* this one. Tiger hit a ball that struck the cart track, bounced so high it hit some tree limbs, then rolled another fifty feet down the track away from the hole. That could have been me!

I'm starting to relate. I draw back the iron there in the TV room, and on the backswing the club unfortunately catches the curtain rod, pulling it down. Just a little café curtain, but it made quite a racket.

"What was that?" Jody yells from the other room.

"Scooter!" I scream, referring to our cat, who is also blamed for foul blustery aromas.

Tiger's cart track–tree shot looked just like mine, except he does not then go on to shoot a 9 on this hole, as I would. He *pars* the son-of-a-bitch!

At this point the announcers pronounce that something is direly wrong with Tiger's game today. On the other hand, the guy *is winning* the tournament, now isn't he?

Tiger yells "Goddamnit!" after one swing—just like me. Glad to see Tiger cursing. Thought he might be an automaton. His profanity-inducing, really bad shot has landed in tall grass, but his recovery shot comes to rest just inches from the hole. The man sure does recover well. I don't recover. I'm terminal.

The announcer says that Tiger's shot from the high grass to the green "redefines courage." Golf announcers say some pretty stupid things when they try to be profound. The announcer trying to wax poetic about Nicklaus passing the baton to Tiger sounds less like a poet laureate than he does like Jack Handy with his Deep Thoughts on *Saturday Night Live*—or a waitress at the IHOP delivering sickening blueberry-pineapple syrup to your table.

The announcers say a lot of things I can't quite comprehend, in large part because they're describing a game so different from the one I try to play. They say things like "putting for the eagle"—things I never hear on the course. They say "an eight-footer for bogey is no fun," when it sounds like a riot to me. They say Phil Mickelson's thirty-foot putt is "certainly makeable" but to me it seems certainly not. When he hits one in a sand trap they say it's "shocking." Why? And they say things like "the second cut [of grass, apparently] is affecting backspin." Could that be *my* problem?

When a player makes a par they lament his "mistake . . . a squandered opportunity." When a thirty-five-foot putt stops two and one half feet from the hole they call it "woefully short." Harsh. And who can putt on such greens? They undulate wildly. Putts break one way, then the other. On one green they go downhill, then sharply uphill, before breaking at a 45 degree angle. Why not toss a couple of windmills and Goofy's nose on the green while you're at it?

I'm sure glad I don't have to play with these guys whispering into microphones about my game. When Fred Funk misses a putt they mutter a mournful "mercy," and when he bogeys a hole they call it "a disaster." (Frankly, a guy named Fred Funk needs no further aggravation.) Sergio García is only 2 under par, so they feel compelled to explain that he has a fever. When Olazabel (the man with the unfortunate middle name "María") chips, they cry "oh noooo!" even though he's chipped onto the green. And winds up shooting a 63!

Davis Love misses the green with a 140-yard iron. "Awwww!" goes the crowd, as the announcer intones: "You wonder how he can hit a shot like that"—meaning "that badly." Hey! Over here! I can answer that.

They jinx people, like Fred Funk, who they call "the greatest driver on the tour" a nanosecond before he whacks one into the woods. They call hole 2 "juicy white-meat" for some reason, and they say things that make absolutely no sense to the bad golfer, like, "He doesn't want to hit it too close to the hole; he wants to be able to take a full swing." *Doesn't want it too close to the hole??!*

The broadcast is all very soothing, conducive to snoozing. I wonder if advertisers get built-in discounts for the snooze factor? Jim Nance, the announcer, has a pacifying, mellifluous voice. If he interjected "Russian ICBMs are scheduled to hit fifty U.S. cities in ten minutes, folks," you'd still remain in your La-Z-Boy to see if Notah Begay made his birdie. And Jim would remain there at the mike to call it for you. (Notah Begay, while sounding like a curried muscle balm, is actually a player on the tour. As is the aforementioned Fred Funk, who sounds like a perpetually depressed cartoon character.)

I hear Jim comment on the fragrance of the flowers, hear him describe shots as "lovely." Does he ever do hockey? Unlike announcers for the NBA or the WWF, for example, golf announcers whisper a lot. They are speaking quietly and reverently, as if in church. The color commentator has an English accent, adding a veneer of sophistication to the proceedings.

The courses are beautiful, the fairways mown in patterns, the greens perfectly smooth, the bunkers brimming with white sand. Flowers bloom. Birds are constantly chirping. None of that damned "CAW-CAWing" I hear in my yard at 6:00 A.M. either, just little tweets and chirps. You can hear the birds so clearly it seems they're either wearing lavalier microphones, or somebody in the truck is "sweetening" the sound with birdcall tapes.

Even the applause, which comes after almost every shot, is soothing, sounding muffled somehow.

Occasionally you hear piano music in the background. Now, where the hell is the piano? Where I play, on ratty public courses, it's more like Dr. Dre on a boom box.

The game of grace and beauty being played before these announcers lends itself to such genteel coverage.

This game is more akin to ballet than the break dancing in water skis style that I play.

These pros hit with beauty and grace, but also with the precision of machines. I recall attending a PGA Seniors tournament, where I stood behind a green looking back down the fairway at tiny, barely perceptible figures hitting golf balls that seconds later somehow plunked down on the green and bit down still. Astonishing! These guys know they hit a certain iron 192 yards—no more, no less—and by God they do, shot after shot. My best guess for that same iron would be, oooh, let's see, somewhere between 35 and 125 yards. If I was in the artillery, I'd wipe out every soldier on our side with "friendly fire."

I see the pros lining up their approach shots on 13 at Valhalla, where their target is a green raised up twenty-two feet and sitting on a wall of rocks surrounded by a moat. And I watch them lofting the balls, and I see the balls gently landing and staying still right in the center of the green. And in that same instant I picture myself hitting a low line drive into that rock wall, and I hear the awful crack, and see the ball ricocheting into the water. I even see my next shot, where the ball overshoots the green and plops down in the water on the other side. I see that all very clearly.

They play a different game. These players don't do doglegs. On the first hole, Tiger doesn't go down the fairway with his first shot, then turn left and go down the dogleg with his second. He cuts the corner, hitting it over the trees so he winds up in the same place after one shot that he would have been after two. If I were playing against him, I would call that cheating. But, then, I wouldn't be, now would I?

A graphic comes on the screen showing Tiger's drives are averaging 308.5 yards. I think they must mean *feet*, because that would work out to about 100 yards, which is a nice drive, in my opinion. The graphic says he hits his drives with 82.1 percent accuracy, whatever that means. Everything is quantified: He has a 61 percent sand save average. I don't even like to keep score.

Scott Dunlap is Tiger's partner! How'd you like to be Tiger's partner, with thousands of people watching you and millions more on TV and you'd never ever won a tournament? Somehow, however, he manages to stay with Tiger the entire round, matching him stroke for stroke, and the announcers refer to him as "the improbable Scott Dunlap." He finishes the day just one stroke behind Tiger, but when I tuned in for the next day of the tournament Scott wasn't listed anywhere among the leaders, and most of them were far, far behind Tiger. Where was Scott? Probably in a Home For Tiger's Partners now, finger-painting and banging his head against the wall.

Davis Love's shot hits a woman. Just like me. Fred Funk hits the crowd. I always thought I'd hate having a gallery of people watch me play, until I realized they act as a human backstop. You hit the ball as hard as you wish and it never goes past the green, it hits people. On the other hand, however, the gallery always goes "awwwwww!" when the pros miss a putt, which is something you say to a baby when it cries, and hearing that repeatedly would definitely make me start flailing away at them with my putter. It would get ugly.

The pros are prima donnas, wimpier than you and I. If a camera clicks when Tiger's lining up his putt, his caddie goes after the guy. Caddies do everything for the pro golfers. They tell them the distance to the pin, windage, suggest what club to use and which way the ball will break on the putt. Would that help me? I'm not sure if any of this information is pertinent to me. I swing, the ball goes . . . somewhere. I do notice that Tiger puts his glove in his right rear pocket when he's putting. I'm definitely going to start doing that.

Tiger pays his caddie, Steve Williams, $600,000 a year or more. Must be a pretty heavy bag. That seems like a lot, except Tiger will be making $900,000 today plus some multiple of that for wearing those Nike swooshes all over his clothes. I figured that the word "Buick" on Tiger's bag probably pays Steve's salary. I figured wrong. Buick is paying Tiger $10 to $15 million over two years to put their name on his bag. Tiger is making $1,742 for every stroke this season. He should swing more, like me.

I snooze . . . and awaken to see Tiger holding another trophy and kissing it. The man may be at risk from silver polish poisoning.

8
Golf 101

I am starting to pick up the language of Golf—and a colorful language it is. Let's try to translate that earlier baffling conversation, shall we?

"I was up and down, but she lipped out on me."

"Up and down" is a phrase meaning to hit an approach shot onto the green and then 1-putt. Good.

"Lipped out" means the putt caught the lip of the cup, twirled a bit, then came out. Bad.

"Chili-dipped the son-of-a-bitch, didn't catch the apron, and rolled right into the pot bunker."

"Chili-dipped" means to hit too much of the ground behind the ball, also known as hitting it "fat" or "sclaffing."

91

"**Apron**" is the short grass, or "frog hair," surrounding the green, you know, like an apron.

"**Pot bunker**" is a deep pot-shaped sand trap.

You see? Now you are learning it, too. Here are some common words and useful phrases for newcomers to the world of Golf:

"**Son-of-a-bitch**"—is commonly heard on the links, with the truncated "Son-of-a . . ." version used at more genteel private golf clubs to avoid receiving letters of reprimand.

"**It's still your turn**"—an annoying phrase you'll be hearing a lot, because the player farthest from the hole always hits next, and often even after 3 consecutive shots "it's still your turn."

"**Away**"—means farthest from the hole. Where you are. Common use: "You're away again, Bill." Common response: "I know, a—hole!"

"**Addressing the ball**"—for real golfers this means taking a stance to hit the ball, but you'll often hear beginners addressing their balls: "You miserable little s%&#!" or "F#@% you!"

"**Fore!**"—you'll be yelling this constantly. It's a warning cry that your ball is about to strike someone. You always shout it too late, and anyway, what are they supposed to do?

"**Gimmee**"—a putt so short your partners say you don't even have to take it. Mafia chieftain Sam "Momo" Giancana was frequently afforded gimmees on puts of forty and fifty feet.

"Irish gimmee"—most gimmees are a few inches, this one is anything within a flag stick's length of the cup.

"Woods" are clubs to golfers, but to us, woods are where we play.

"Hole-in-one"—not applicable to your game. Nor are: "honors," "eagle," "birdie," or "par."

"Bogey"—one over par, a long-term goal.

"Double bogey"—aka a "buzzard"—an attainable goal.

"Triple bogey"—think of it as your par.

"Deep grass squirt"—those shots that go five feet in tall grass. Often in succession.

"Topped dribble"—also known as a chopper, a short bouncer, another part of your "short game."

"Knick knack paddy wack"—percussive sounds your ball makes ricocheting deep in the woods.

"Whiff"—when you swing and miss. We call it a practice shot, real golfers count it as a stroke.

"Pitch"—for golfers a short wedge shot to the green. For us it's literally a pitch of the ball either under- or over-handed.

"Hand wedge"—what you use for pitch shots. Also, "hand mashie" or "five-finger iron."

"Sand hand wedge"—blasting out of sand by tossing ball and a handful of sand for authenticity.

"Foot wedge"—novices are allowed "free kicks" in golf.

"Bisque"—an agreed-to extra shot.

"Bisquick"—rapid extra unagreed-upon shot taken before others notice.

"Mashie"—5-iron. (Also, stepping on opponent's ball, making it almost impossible to hit.)

"Baffing spoon"—9-iron.

"Mashie niblick"—7-iron.

"Smashie da-stick"—breaking club over knee.

"Bashie dose-pricks"—group behind you hits a ball into your group, you tee it up and bash it back at them.

"Crashie"—your ball hits waiter carrying full tray in patio dining area.

"Gashie"—your ball hits another player in forehead.

"Flashie"—your ball hits a series of objects with one shot (e.g., cart–tree–partner).

"Gnashie"—club member's teeth grinding when he realizes he could be thrown out for inviting you.

"Rashie"—woman who relieves herself in woods and uses poison sumac to tidy up.

"Splashie"—ball hit into club swimming pool, soup, or beverage.

"Relief"—rules helping golfers out of sticky situations, or what we get in bushes.

"Nearest point of relief" is where you drop your ball or your pants.

"Break"—contour of the green or what car windows do when we play.

"A day at the beach"—taking three or more shots to get out of sand trap.

"Fade"—an intentional slice by a skilled player. Useful in implying that your shot into that condominium on the right was intentional: "I'd been meaning to get together with those folks for some time."

"Draw"—an intentional hook. Useful in implying that you were trying to hit it into that cupholder in the Chevy Tahoe.

"Sandy"—when a real golfer hits out of the bunker and 1-

putts. Or, when we hit it from one bunker across the green into another bunker.

"**Wormburner**"—bad golfer's constant companion, usually a fairway wood shot that races through, while never completely losing touch with, the grass.

"**Duck hook**"—another weapon in the bad golfer's arsenal, a plunging hook, similar to a "Snappy Tom."

"**Free drop**"—the legal dropping of your ball elsewhere after it has landed in, for example, ground under repair.

"**Pocket drop**"—hole golfers cut in a front pants pocket from which they discreetly make illegal ball drops down their pant legs after yelling, "Oh here's my ball in the fairway!"

"**Unplayable lie**"—you saying you found your ball in the cup.

"**You didn't club me right**"—an important phrase for bad golfers. Used to blame caddies for suggesting the wrong club and causing our poor shots.

"**Taxiing**"—picking up ball and driving it to green in cart.

9

Country Clubbed

I've been invited to play golf at an exclusive private country club!

I know I'm not ready for this caliber of play or social interaction. But I accept, drawn by the thought that maybe I could beat women. Little women. Little middle-aged women.

Diane invited me. She is a woman not much over five feet tall, and while still quite attractive and girlish-looking, is really just a few years younger than me. Maybe I could beat her. She invited me to play golf with her, and with two other women, one of whom was Val, who isn't all that big either, and who had complained recently of a rotator cuff problem. So maybe I could beat her. Unfortunately, the third woman turned out to be Rick, Diane's husband. Apparently the third woman in our foursome decided it might be too dangerous to play with me. She has children to think of.

Diane's club carries an aura of distinction, formality, and history. It seems to have been founded about the time the *Mayflower* landed and our nation's first white families waded ashore in their golf spikes. That's the feeling you get when you drive up the club's long, winding, tree-lined driveway, past the sign proudly proclaiming the founding date, then past a forbidding "Members Only" sign, where you half expect a checkpoint with armed guards doing blueblood tests and asking if your mother was in the DAR. The golf course itself is ranked among the finest in the New York area, and many of golf's all-time greats have played here over the years. It costs more than $50,000 to join—and, no, you can't.

This would be my first golfing experience at a real country club, although I did make out with my girlfriend on a green during a ninth-grade dance at our local club, and enjoyed that very much until the automatic sprinkler system came on. Not mine, the golf course's.

Preparing for the big day at Diane's club, I must admit I was a bit nervous, about my golf, and about my manners (etiquette does not come naturally to me), and, you know, just being *clean* enough and everything to pass muster. The club's a bit stuffy. Old school. Once after several hours of drinking and dancing at a wedding reception there, I removed my tuxedo jacket only to have a sentry rush over and instruct me to put it back on. Later, however, another guest would remove his slacks on the dance floor, which certainly took some of the pressure off me.

What to wear? Would this be black tie optional golf? I frantically dig through several closets before finding my pair of white golf shoes, which are fashioned from rich,

Corinthian polyvinyl chloride, the ones someone gave to me absolutely free (and at a cost to them of at least $9.95). But, are white golf shoes like . . . gay? I wondered. These are the kinds of things novices just don't know. I'd heard that loud pink and green plaid polyester pants are no longer the thing, so I threw on my newest polo shirt, a light golfy sweater, and a pair of khakis—turning on all the bedroom lights to ensure my WASPy duds were spotless.

A member had lent me her club rule book to peruse before my visit: "Male golfers must wear shirts with collars at all times," it instructed, and at a place like this, that could mean even in the shower. So I definitely ruled out my "Let's Go Met's" T-shirt (the one I'd worn to renew my vows). You've got to *blend*.

Club rules stated: "Golf shorts may be worn; however, jeans, brief shorts, or 'cutoffs' are not permitted." That seemed semireasonable, although some jeans look a hell of a lot better than some of the flammable golf slacks you see out on the course. "Brief shorts" are underwear, aren't they? And cutoffs I pretty much reserve for mowing the lawn and Saturday nights at the Ponderosa with the missus. Some clubs don't allow shorts at all.

The rules are even tougher on women: "Female golfers must wear golf dresses, skirts, culottes, slacks, or Bermuda length shorts. Brief skirts, brief shorts, tank tops, or jeans of any description are NOT permitted." The club really hates jeans—even if they're $300 Versaces. Some members recently wanted to loosen up and have a square dance, so they petitioned the board for a denim exemption for one night only and were flatly refused. Do-si-do in your tux-e-do.

Too bad about no miniskirts on the golf course, but men say it is difficult to putt when you're excited—mentally *or* physically (see the Rules of Golf under "Obstructions"). I've been told of officials at other clubs measuring a woman's shorts to find that they were more than an inch and a half above the knee, and ordering her to leave.

But there are even more pressing issues for me. Like, no clubs. I still don't own any clubs. (Not to mention, no game. I still don't really have a golf game.)

My wife isn't home so I decide I'll use her clubs—appropriate, I think, for me to play with women's clubs when playing against women. I'm walking out the door when I notice that all but three clubs are still wrapped in bubble plastic because they've never been used. Not good. I tear at the wrapped clubheads with my fingers and teeth, spitting little bits of bubble plastic on the living room carpet. I also remove the tags from the new golf bag, as well as the brown paper stuffing in its zipper pockets.

When you drive in, right after the "Members Only" sign, there's one reading "Valet Parking Only." A Mercedes—bus? No, it's a huge sedan—and a big BMW are right behind me. It's like the Berlin Auto Show. My car's imported, but from a country that more or less sat out World War II. Also it's a year old. And leased. Can they tell? Is it okay? Luckily, I'd gone all the way with the Super Deluxe Package at the car wash a few days before—with carnauba wax and the "New Car" fragrance freshener.

Pulling under the porte cochere, a lad leaps out the

front door of the club, starts calling me "sir," unloads my golf bag, then speeds off in my car. He has either accepted it for parking or he's trying to get it off the premises as fast as he can. I've witnessed the latter when someone drives a Ford Fiesta up to the front door of the Beverly Hills Hotel.

Another fellow hustles off—somewhere—with my wife's clubs. Where is he taking them? I recall the story of valet parking attendants at a restaurant in Florida who were not affiliated with the restaurant but rather with a stolen car ring. A victim was quoted in the paper as saying he didn't give a damn about his car, but his new set of golf clubs was in the trunk.

The guy in the car right behind me happens to be a friend, John, who shows me to the pro shop and starter's area. "I didn't know you played," he says. "I don't," I reply. We pass through the bar, and the liquor looks delicious, and quite necessary, but we keep moving.

John points out at the course. "I got a hole-in-one right over there," he says with a laugh. "Yeah, I teed off on that hole over there and hooked it onto the practice putting green and it went in the hole." I'm glad to hear it, glad to know my brand of golf has been seen here before.

Bill, the golf pro, is friendly. He's just had lasik eye surgery, which he says could take more strokes off my game. (Lasik Eye Surgery: -3 strokes, that's a total of minus 62!). A friend suggests I take a lesson from Bill. "He's great if you're at a 9 and want to get to a 3," my friend says. Sounds good until I realize he's not talking about going from 9 shots *per hole* to 3 shots per hole—

something I'd love to do—but, rather, from a 9 *handicap* to a 3.

We meet Dave, the starter, sort of an air traffic controller of the golf course. This course has twenty-seven holes, and I ask him if he could sort of hide me somewhere out there. But golf is too popular these days for that. He's giving me a break just letting me play. If he sizes up a foursome and decides they'll delay other golfers, he can keep them off the course altogether—and at this point I'd probably tip him handsomely to do just that.

According to club rules, however, it's ultimately the members' duty to have knowledge of "the ability of invited guests . . . members are responsible for the conduct, appearance, etiquette, and speed of play of their guests." Yikes. My friends are really going out on a limb, bringing me here.

Then, Dave turns to me and says, simply, "Brian will be your caddie."

Sweet Jesus! A caddie!

I've never had a caddie before. Aren't they all these young guys who are great players and who kind of hold in their guffaws and then make fun of you later back in the caddie shack? Yes. There's a course in North Carolina that uses llamas as caddies, probably because they can't talk.

I don't need a caddie. I don't deserve a caddie. Like Slobodan Milosevic, I don't want any observers around as witnesses to my atrocities. In this case, misery does not love company.

But guess what? During prime time on the course, you *must* have a caddie—as a service to you, the golfer, yes, but also to keep your sorry butt moving. Even if you rent a cart, if there are caddies available, you have to use them. In fact, "no golfer playing before 3:00 P.M. is permitted to carry his/her golf bag." Could I play with one club, no bag?

I'm getting nervous. I look on the information board, which tells me that the weather is threatening and the grass is .468 inches high.

.468! These golfers are so good they need to know the grass length to the thousandth of an inch? Ay-yi-yi! Well, I say by now it's .471 at least. More pertinent to me, the rough is three inches.

Brian is two-bagging it for Val and me. Diane and Rick are in a cart. We head for the first tee.

Maybe I can beat the women. Diane and Val are not supercompetitive types, and they each have a sense of humor about all this. Diane says one time when she and her sister played here she laughed so hard she wet her pants, had to wrap a jacket around herself, and drive home to change.

I've had a couple of previous golf experiences with Val. We played mini-golf with our spouses at the Jersey Shore, and I held my own despite her home course advantage. And once on a vacation the four of us were lying on the beach in Carmel, when a ball came flying off a cliff on the Pebble Beach course and hit the side of her sunglasses. It was the part that sticks out in front that wasn't touching her head, so she was fine, but both lenses shot out into the water. I took a photograph of her with a ball in her eye socket in case we decided to sue. So I felt I knew a little bit about her game.

Before the first drive, the excuses begin. Rick has a

cold, Val that rotator cuff injury, Diane already has to go to the bathroom, and me, well, my excuse is I don't frigging play the damned game!

Rick, a powerfully built guy, goes first and hits a nice drive. No, actually, it's going into the water there on the right. All right Rick! My man! Diane very loudly counts "oooonnne," as he tees up his second opening drive. Practice makes perfect, and his second drive is much better.

Then it's my turn. I've seen a golf club manufacturers' survey showing that 41 million more people would play golf were it not for their embarrassment on that damned first tee.

But my first problem today is . . . I don't have a ball, such an important part of the game. Val has extras. "How many extras?" I ask. "Plenty," she says. I doubt that. She's never played with me before.

I even *look* bad at the tee. I don't just gracefully bend down and stick the tee in the ground and balance the ball on top all in one motion. I squat and use both hands, sort of like I'm doing some complicated gardening function. And I really have no idea how far down in the ground the tee is supposed to go.

I stand up and look down the fairway like they do on TV, and quite frankly, I don't like what I see. I see a sizable pond to the right, and—through those trees there— the Red Lobster restaurant on the left. I am fully capable of hitting both, although probably not with the same shot. I envision claws and bibs and melted butter flying; it could be bad. I see a lot of sand looming off in the distance and menacing stands of trees. Rumor has it that they're making the course a tad easier, to accommodate a PGA Seniors tournament scheduled to come here, but to me it looks like the course was designed by the same krauts who did the defenses at Omaha Beach. Where's the love?

Since there's no defense or even an opponent in golf, instead there are hazards—which other sports do not have. Wouldn't it be interesting if there were water hazards and sand traps on a hockey rink or a basketball court? Or a big tree in center field at Yankee Stadium?

The only good news for us bad golfers is that hazards are put where they are in order to trap decent golfers. We always hit short of the traps, although we do often catch them on our second or third shots.

Most hazards are trees, sand, or water—although not always those intended by designers. My brother-in-law placed two successive wood shots into a crowded swimming pool at a country club where he was a guest. Adjoining condos are also hazards, and rules vary about playing balls off patios, guests at barbecues, and coffee tables.

And there are regional peculiarities. Eighty cows roam a course in Nebraska. Hit into a pie, you get a free drop. Goose poop is a hazard on courses almost everywhere now—despite the best efforts of dogs and noise cannons and what have you to make the lazy things fly south instead of lounging around up here performing their vital excretory function. No one has tried semiautomatic machine gun fire, however, which I favor. At The Florida Club, we found the stench of pigs next door to be a monumental hazard. There's a feud with the pig farmer, who has taken to buying more and more pigs and using large fans to blow the stench at golfers.

Black bears roam the courses of Pennsylvania and elsewhere. Coyotes, too. Crows fly off with balls. Lions are seen on the links in Kenya, crocodiles in Zambia, gators in Florida. In Zimbabwe you get a free drop if your ball goes into a mortar crater, and at the course along the Demilitarized Zone in Korea, hooks go into real minefields. You can bet if the balls are expensive ones, golfers go right in there after them.

Despite the rising hazard anxiety, the golfer must go on. Standing here at the first tee, I demonstrate complete knowledge of *my* game, if not *the* game, by confidently predicting—based on my experience at the driving range a few days earlier—that I will, in fact, be slicing the ball into the pond on the right, with a 10 percent chance I'll hit a little chopper to the left at a 45 degree angle about twenty-five feet from the tee.

I draw back that driver, trying to remember all two hundred things that Liz told me in the gym, but as I bring it forward something comes over me, a flush of unease and a premonition that this is going to turn out badly.

I look up—too soon!—to see the drive rising high and with a fair amount of distance but beginning to tail off a bit to the right . . . and a bit more now . . . and . . . yes, we have splashdown, Mission Control, in the pond, about five feet offshore. Just as I'd predicted.

It is suggested I try another tee shot, which I am happy to do, and this one bounces to the left at about a 45 degree angle, coming to rest about forty feet away from the tee. As predicted.

We have already broken a course rule: "The taking of a mulligan on the first tee is not permitted."

It is here that Rick reminds me of the old golf custom that when a man hits a drive that does not reach the ladies' tee, he is to pull down his pants and leave them that way until reaching the green. My second tee shot so qualifies. Diane says that when she and her sister were paired with two strangers on a public course in Nantucket, one of the men hit just such a short shot and when they informed him of the old custom, he informed them that he was Senator Christopher Dodd of Connecticut and really couldn't afford to play along. Presidents are so much more fun than senators.

Sooo, I elect to play the first shot, the splasher. The one at the bottom of the pond is the better lie. Brian gives me a ball, tells me to stand a club's length from the pond and drop the ball from shoulder height into the 3.0-inch rough.

He hands me an iron of some kind, which I use to advance the ball about ten feet. Obviously it's his fault; the ignoramus gave me the wrong club. So, it can be good to have a caddie. To blame.

There are at least two schools of thought on caddies. A group called the Bad Golfers Association discourages their use on the theory that they prevent you from cheating, e.g., finding your ball in the woods when you don't want to, catching you kicking the ball, and so on.

However, a caddie I spoke to says just the opposite is true: He'll run on ahead, and to keep you happy and to keep the game moving so he can go back and play cards, he'll be sure to do whatever's necessary to ensure a nice lie.

"Hey," he reminds, "you're paying us." Then he held out his hand.

The servant thing is bothersome. Caddies are often treated poorly, although, here again, quite the opposite can be true. One former caddie I know parlayed his contacts with successful businessmen he caddied for into acceptance at a fine university, an internship at a major investment banking house, tutelage in starting up his own Internet Web site, and a $20 million profit when he sold it at age twenty-two. He is now a member of the country club where a couple of years ago he was caddieing! It's like the French Revolution, with the caddies taking over the club.

Despite Brian's best efforts, that problem of hitting little squibs would haunt me all day. Too many shots in which the ball goes ten feet. Except near the green, where I'd like to hit the ball ten feet onto the green and instead the ball goes thirty feet *over* it. Often my ten-foot shot is a warm-up, as it were, for my next shot, which seems to always go just about where I wanted the one before it to go. And that one stroke, which can turn a 7 into a 6, makes all the difference between a truly terrible golfer and a merely hideous one.

The rest of my first-hole golfing experience goes well, by my standards, and I wind up with a 6 or 7. I can't really remember. I'm blocking. I will be at 6s and 7s all day, but—hey!—I'm staying off adjoining thoroughfares and not hitting from the Hooters parking lot.

On the second hole, Brian suggests I keep my left arm straighter and not lift my head so soon. He is very diplomatic, saying things that are meant to be positive, like,

"That's okay, you're advancing the ball." As opposed to what? "Retreating the ball"? I can do that, too.

Using his golf tips, I hit a decent drive followed by a nice 5-wood. Val takes the opportunity to compliment me, saying "You're not bad despite your shitty shoes."

And I actually believe Jody's new, technologically advanced clubs are helping a little, perhaps turning my frighteningly bad shots into merely poor ones.

"That was poor, Bill."

"Thanks, Rick."

My short game lets me down, as I chop-chop-chop my way to the green using the P (for Pathetic) wedge again—and again—and again. For a 7. Val helpfully gives me a string with beads on it for counting my strokes, sort of a pocket abacus. But it only has ten beads.

On the third hole—which is another 6 or 7 for me—putting becomes a major concern. Val remembers that I was a better putter at mini-golf. So I ask her to stand between my ball and the hole with her legs spread and her arms waving like a windmill, and you know, it does help.

But I am not beating the little middle-aged women. And it's starting to irk me that they get to tee off twenty yards ahead of me, on the red women's tees, when they are clearly better. Why do *they* get the advantage? This is the twenty-first century for chrissake. You want equality, I'll give you equality . . . get your butts back here and tee off with us! No! Wait! We'll move forward.

Diane is far better than me, and Val is only clearly better. I do manage to tie her on a few holes, largely because she and Diane have already played eighteen holes of golf this morning and are beat. Rick is having an inconsistent round, hitting some truly great shots and some not so great. He has begun getting down on himself, taking shots and saying things like: "The only two good balls I hit all day were when I stepped on the rake in the sand trap."

To add spice to their games, Rick and Diane don't play for money, but for even higher stakes. They play "Your Wish Is My Command" golf, which means the winner can command the loser to do anything, which used to be pretty racy. But after playing like this for many, many years, the couple came home from a round of golf one day and the loser, Diane, said: "What do you want me to do, big boy?" Or words to that effect.

"Well," Rick replied, "I'd really like you to wash my car."

"Our marriage is over!" cried Diane.

The most discernible pattern emerging here is that it's usually my turn. The person farthest from the hole—the person who is "away"—always hits next, and that always seems to be me. You really get your money's worth when you're bad. Not like other sports, where you sit on the bench when you're bad and don't get to play at all.

Make no mistake about it, while many great pros have played here, this old course has seen some nasty shots. One golfer hit a shot into the men's locker room here, prompting his partner to run in shouting, "Clear the way, he's playing through!" (Which has been done in tournament play at another club, by the way, where the golfer opened the window and hit it back out.)

John hit that hole-in-one over on the practice putting green, and any number of duffers have put one in the swimming pool or into the seafood salad on the patio during lunch. I am part of a great heritage.

One player was hit by a ball in the balls and was seriously injured here. He eventually lost a testicle. The other three players in his foursome lay him down by the side of the fairway and kept playing. Hey, tee times are tough to get on weekends. Golfers understand.

I slice my next shot into a stand of trees. Brian informs me that since I'd have to stand on the cart path to play the shot, thereby possibly becoming a hit-and-run victim, I get to drop my ball again in a spot a bit farther off the path. Unfortunately he won't let me drop it on the fairway side—nor will he hold back the branches of, nor prune any limbs from, a large tree staring me in the face.

Even so, Brian and I are bonding. He says encouraging things like "You could be a lot worse."

"Gee, thanks, Bri."

"Some guys miss shots and break their clubs over their knees," he says. "One throws his putter back at the bag when he misses, and of course we're wearing the bags on our shoulders."

By the 7th hole I am ready to lie down by the side of the fairway. I am already tiring, I hate to say. But of course I've already taken a lot of shots, and I've walked one hell of a lot farther than the others, taking serpentine paths, tacking this way and that, zigzagging my way from tee to green.

"This one is bad," Rick warns as we approach the next tee. "It makes you want to crush your clubs. Put 'em right in the ol' car crusher. Still in your car." I slice my shot into a gorgeous flowering crabapple, creating a dazzling floral spray.

It *is* beautiful out here, in late April, with the flowering trees and bushes and the buds on the trees. A hawk flies over. Brian points it out and says foxes and even a coyote have been spotted on the course. A wildlife refuge to be sure, right here in New Jersey in a suburb better known for its myriad species of shopping malls. Too bad Audubon didn't get a chance to paint the Garden State Mall.

On the 8th, talk begins to turn away from golf to cocktails and what *kinds* of cocktails we are going to have when we finish. The gimmee putts suddenly become twice as long as before.

The 9th green is adjacent to the club, on purpose, allowing golfers to relieve themselves in clubhouse rest rooms before setting off on the back 9, thereby reducing the assessments necessary for new shrubs. It also allows golfers like ourselves to . . . just . . . quit.

As we approach the green, I ask Brian which club he'd recommend and if he'd mind going into the club and closing the drapes so people inside can't see me play. I also feel the curtains might provide another measure of safety for patrons in the bar and dining room.

I don't know what my final tally is and I don't ask. Club rules specify you must post your scores for 18 holes, but not 9. Since most of my scores were 6s or 7s I figure my score was probably around 60.

It's a good day. As a guest I can't buy drinks or dinner even if I want to—it's all on the monthly tab.

To sum up, I finish fourth. I don't beat any little

women, but I don't lose *any* balls (thanks to Brian), except that very first one that went in the water. I receive no citations for dress code violations. I don't hit anybody. I don't throw any clubs, pee on any bushes, and I keep the ball off surrounding thoroughfares and hit no houses.

Damnit, I'm getting *good.*

10

Mind If I Join You?

Maybe I should join a club. A country club.

Sure, they're stodgy and expensive, but how else can you *play* this stupid game? Unless you enjoy sleeping in your car to get tee times at public courses, you're almost forced to join one.

One morning I drive over to the Metedeconk National Golf Club, its stately private clubhouse fronting a fantastic Robert Trent Jones 27-hole course.

Driving in, I see no guard towers, no concertina wire, no checkpoints, and no aggressive valet parkers trying to carjack me—so it all seems rather casual, open, friendly. I stride briskly up the front steps, hoping to stay a step ahead of the radar, half expecting a couple of burly Secret Service types with walkie-talkie cords in their ears to grab me. But none do. So, I take a survey stroll through the dining room and bar area—very nice—then step confidently to the front desk and ask the receptionist:

"Do you have an application form?"

She gives me a quizzical look: "Are you seeking employment?"

Not good. I thought I was blending rather well, but this shakes my confidence.

"Uh, no, not really," I reply. "I mean, membership forms. Applications for membership."

"One moment please," she says, picking up the phone to speak to someone—hopefully not Security: What if she has one of those red buttons under her desk like the bank tellers have?

"Mr. Bechert," she says into the phone, "we have a gentleman here asking about membership."

Chip Bechert, a most amiable, fortyish man, dressed "resort casual" and ready to hit the links at a moment's notice, bounds into the lobby to greet me warmly and invite me to sit down for an iced tea. Things are back on track, going rather swimmingly, don't you think?

Chip, the director of membership, casually asks what I'm looking for in a golf club, and I tell him "a course."

"Do you play a lot?" he asks.

"Oh, not really," I say, "I'm new to the game."

"What's your handicap?" he asks.

"None," I reply. Why? Did I wrongly park in a marked spot in the lot? I didn't want him to think he was going to have to build a ramp or anything.

He's referring to my golf handicap, which has never been calculated, but is severe and possibly inoperable: "I shoot about a 110," I say, lying. It's probably more like a 125, really, and on this challenging course more like a 175. I look around the course later, and see that it is at once uncommonly beautiful and fraught with perils such as I'd never seen before, perils like *double* doglegs. Long ones. We're not talking dachshunds here.

And you do have to put your golf handicap on your application! "It's okay if it's high," he insists, "although if you tell me you're shooting a 125 [which I hadn't], I would certainly tell you all about our fine practice facility and the hours our golf pro gives lessons."

"Do you belong to other clubs?" he asks. I can't think of any. I told him we joined BJ's Price Club, a discount store, and the AARP sent me a temporary membership card, unsolicited, when I turned fifty. The bastards.

Whether or not there's a waiting list is difficult to determine, but one more answer out of me like the 110, and I think the answer is "yes" and "long."

Never join a club until you find out about the food, a (fat) friend had advised me. I ask, and Chip says it's "great"—although "great" food at a country club is usually like "great" food at a pet motel. Furthermore, he says there's no annual or monthly minimum you have to spend, unlike almost every other club I've ever heard of. Generally my wife and I are treated to the hospitality of our friends belonging to country clubs on the thirtieth or thirty-first of the month, when said friends take us to their clubs to try to eat up to those minimums: "Another chateaubriand, Bill?" The worst part of these minimums is that they can't be used for alcoholic beverages.

"Not to be crass," I ask, "but what may I ask are the fees for joining this club?"

"Fifty-five hundred," he replies. Not *bad!* Not bad at all. I'm thinking "sign me up."

"That is the annual fee," he continues. "The initial membership fee is . . . one twenty-five."

One twenty-five. Let's see. He is saying "one twenty-five" in much the same way the auctioneers do at Sotheby's, or the clerks at Tiffany, so that you just *know* he's not talking one hundred twenty-five anything except *thousands!*

I am tempted to tell him what I once told a hotel desk clerk who quoted me a room rate of $200 when I was on a family vacation looking for a room with a roll-a-way for around thirty-five bucks: "I'm sorry, we were looking for something a little nicer," I said, and walked out.

But he notes that we're getting a little ahead of the game, that I have to be sponsored by at least three members of the club and that membership is by invitation only—and so far he hasn't really extended me one per se.

I blink first. "I fold," I say. I'm out. I'm holding a pair of deuces over here and he's talking royal flush or better to open.

This seems to relieve him greatly. We both relax. He tells me I'm what he calls a "walk-in," few if any of whom have ever become members of this club. "I try to be courteous to everyone," he says, "but for some of these people the fees might be more than they paid for their houses. When I break it to them, they start to sense that they just might be in the wrong place." We've all been there.

But Chip notes that members here get back 80 percent of their *one twenty-five* when they leave the club. Members of clubs elsewhere in the area say their clubs initially charge substantially less—say, $20,000 or $40,000—but many of the clubs keep it all. There are other clubs charging as much as $200,000 or more to join, and one nouveau riche magnet in the area has charged as much as $320,000!

In New York's suburbs initiation fees tend to run in the neighborhood of $10,000 to $50,000, with a $10,000 to $15,000 (refundable) bond on top of that, plus annual dues of $5,000 to $10,000, possibly an annual assessment of a thousand or two, and sometimes monthly service charges, as well as annual dining room minimums up to $1,800, and even locker fees.

He says people wanting to join often drop names and claim to know club members. "We check that, of course," he says, "and sometimes their knowing people is not good. Sometimes the members they know wish they didn't. One said: 'Yes I know him and if he joins, I'm out.'"

If they say they're members of other clubs, Chip calls the other clubs. He'll go to their offices or homes to have in-depth face-to-face interviews. He swears he doesn't check your voting record and doesn't ask about political persuasions, although making bombs in the basement would be a red flag in the country club milieu. He does ask what schools you went to, about volunteer work to satisfy the character issue, and certainly about your business background.

You don't even *see* an application form until you've passed muster. Members at other clubs say their applications required bank account numbers, their spouse's financial records, driving records, family photographs, and as many as seven letters of recommendation from other members. Sponsors often have to fill out questionnaires, asking, for example, what percent of their total business is done with the applicant and how many hours they have spent with the applicant and his family in a social setting.

At one club, an applicant was completely qualified for membership except his very successful business was in the field not of stocks and bonds, but of *bail* bonds, and since other members might be uneasy about the prospect of his entertaining manslaughterers and other such clients here, and since "Jersey Bail Bonds" kind of stuck out like a sore thumb there on the ol' application, it was just listed as "JBB Ltd." He sailed through.

No essay is required, and certainly no Scholastic Aptitude Test. It's always a little disconcerting to meet people at country clubs who are well established and well-to-do, yet could not possibly answer the $100 question ("What color is your shirt?") on *Who Wants to Be a Millionaire?* That, like "Vice President Dan Quayle," indicates something's wrong with the system.

The process tends to favor older people who've enjoyed some success. I have seen actual *dead people* playing gin rummy at country clubs—I'm pretty sure. I went to a country club New Year's Eve party that started breaking up around 11:15 as I recall. And at another club, the introductory tour pretty much revolved around a twenty-minute demonstration of their new portable defibrillator.

Chip puts together the dossier on an applicant, and presents it to the twelve members of the board who make their decision. All of this is, of course, way more than most adoption agencies go through when you ask for a child, but not as much as they do at some clubs.

At many clubs there's a far more tortuous route. Applicants might be placed on a ten-year waiting list.

They might be subjected to a "*Mayflower* check" of their bloodlines. It's enough to make you write on the application that you once received oral sex from a member of the Junior League.

The name of the country club applicant might be posted on a bulletin board for sixty days, inviting negative comments. In some clubs if there's *one* objector, one blackball, for any reason, the applicant is turned away. Too loud, too tacky, too "ethnic," too racy, too whatever. Thumbs-down. At one club, attempts at membership failed when an applicant's son beat up the son of a board member at school, and another applicant was turned down when he was recognized as the guy who'd defeated a particularly competitive board member at racquetball.

But it gets more humiliating than that. At many clubs, the couple wishing to join is invited over for a visual inspection by the membership committee. At one local club a prospective member was told by his sponsor to tell his wife to "dress like a nun and keep her mouth shut," good advice at a club where couples wishing to join have been crushed when they were turned down because the wife's skirt was too short or she mispronounced a word.

"I weed out the applications," Chip says. "There's plenty of money out there, you have to find people who get along."

"People who get along" is not code. Metedeconk has a diverse membership. But it certainly *is* code at many private clubs, which have the constitutional right to let in and keep out anyone they wish. There are still all-male clubs, all-white clubs, all-black clubs, all-WASP clubs, all-gentile clubs, all-Jewish clubs, all-Japanese clubs, and even an all-female club or two.

It's perfectly legal. At many clubs, women cannot become full members, cannot set foot in certain club areas, and are not allowed on the golf course at certain (prime) times. At one, a woman going to the bar unescorted to order a drink has brought a letter of reprimand from club officers. Women in shorts that don't fall to a prescribed distance from their knees are told to change. A woman who brought a sandwich from home for her child was reprimanded, as was a woman whose suit was thought too revealing. It seems that clubs allowing women want them to at least look like men.

One Long Island club has drawn a line on the floor in the bar area, sort of a quarantine zone, behind which sit two tables for women. At that club, there's been a ruling that men may, in an emergency, pee in the bushes, but that women have no such right. The ruling apparently did not address the issue of where, in an emergency, a woman *was* allowed to pee, but I would think some Depends in the golf bag might be a good idea.

Excuse me, is this *Iran?*

There are still clubs that allow no women at all—not as members, and not even on the *grounds!* Women must drop off their husbands or their (male) children for golf lessons at the gate. Years ago, a Long Island club that banned women was holding a golf tournament, and women were somehow allowed to come and watch, but when it started to rain and some of them sought shelter in the clubhouse things got ugly between members who thought that was okay in an emergency and those who did not. Zero Tolerance. Women madder than wet hens were everywhere. An emergency board meeting was called and a simple solution was found: no more golf tournaments.

In clubs where women are allowed in, it's often grudgingly. At an old prestigious club in suburban Westchester, a husband and wife who were not getting along at all and on the verge of divorce had to make an untimely appearance before the membership committee to be inspected. There were five committee members rotating around the roomful of candidates, each member spending ten minutes with the various couples.

One member asked the husband why he wanted to join and the husband is said by an observer to have laid it on thick about the status of the venerable club and what he could add as a member and what an honor it would be to join.

Then the inspector general turned to the wife and asked the same question, to which she replied:

"I think golf is for assholes."

Okay. Having no further questions, the interrogator moved on upstairs with his colleagues to compare notes and decide which applicants would be receiving invitations to join.

Meanwhile, the couple left the building to scream at each other in the parking lot, all the way home, and throughout the evening.

Their phone rang, and it was the club member who'd sponsored them calling. The husband began a steady stream of apologies that went on for several minutes during which time the sponsor kept trying to break in.

"No, no, no!" said the sponsor. "Wait a minute, wait a minute! You don't understand. You're in!"

"Whaaat?" said the husband. "How?"

"They know she'll never *play!*" answered the sponsor. The club really didn't like women around—particularly on the golf course.

Once you somehow gain acceptance to a club, you have to mind your Ps and Qs. The aforementioned letters of reprimand can fly for the slightest infraction. A letter was sent to a local club to a member whose guest wore a shirt that was deemed too loud. Moreover, you can not only be reprimanded but thrown out. "If, for example, you had one too many drinks and took your shirt off at the big Fourth of July party," says one club member, "you would not only be thrown out of the club but so would your sponsor!"

So why join a country club? Because you love to play golf, and you want to play when you want to play, and the private courses are usually a lot nicer, and so is the ambience. A lot of people like the sense of belonging, too, of going to a place where they're welcome and known by all. Not to mention, many don't allow cell phones.

But be careful. You can be kicked out for the slightest infraction. No matter *who* you are! Take O.J. Simpson, you know, the former Buffalo Bills football star? C'mon, you remember him. He was kicked out of a country club just down the road for some darned thing. I never did hear what it was.

11

Among My Own Kind

Maybe we should try to join some place a little more *relaxed.*

Maybe here, at Goat Hill: euphemistically called the Shelter Island (public) Country Club. I've stopped by a few times. It seems clearly the type of place I belong (although I would have joined a Michigan club advertising "18 Holes For $18 & Free Six-Pack" if it weren't so inconvenient).

Here at Goat Hill, there are pickup trucks in the parking lot, something you don't see at a lot of other country clubs. Guys in jeans and T-shirts sit at the small bar drinking Bud, not cosmopolitans. Although they appear to be grounds-keepers assistants or maintenance personnel, they are actually golfers and in all probability *members*. The local bon vivants (many of them in yellow "Shelter Island Fire Department" T-shirts) tell jokes and tales of emergency plumbing mishaps they're supposed to be fixing for clients but aren't. There are tables and plastic chairs. Food is served and it's supposed to be pretty good since Phil took over, having been stolen away from the Four Seasons or somewhere. The pro shop is a converted closet.

The clubhouse is quaint, an old, slightly out-at-the-elbows, gray-shingled, white-trimmed Nantuckety-looking structure, sitting on perhaps the highest point on Shelter Island in eastern Long Island, offering vistas over the treetops of a small harbor filled with boats to the north and a large bay to the south. It has a nice wraparound porch filled with tables for diners and drinkers, protected by heavy mesh wire that detracts somewhat from the appearance, rather like a bug screen on a Cadillac grille or plastic covers on the living room couch—but it *saves lives!*

On the Fourth of July they park cars on the fairways. There are deer and sometimes deer *hunters* on the course. How's *that* for a hazard? Carts are allowed anywhere, and it probably wouldn't matter much if you just drove your car from hole to hole.

We have contacts here. Jerry Brennan, the guy with the used golf ball stand across the street, is president and membership chairman of the Shelter Island Country Club. That ought to tell you something. Usually presidents of country clubs don't sell used golf balls in their front yards, they sell things like stocks and bonds on Wall Street.

We stop by his "Previously Owned Golf Ball Emporium" on our way home from golfing at Goat Hill to tell him that tonight is going to be a sensational one for hawking used balls out on the course thanks to the two dozen we just lost playing 9 holes, and to ask him about joining.

"Would you sponsor us?" I ask, knowing if we had him for a sponsor we were as good as *in!*

"Sponsor you?" Jerry asks. "You mean give you money to put my name on your hat?" Apparently they don't require sponsors.

"What would it take to become a member here, Jerry?" I ask. "How many letters of recommendation will I need?" Again he doesn't know what I'm talking about.

"References," I say. "Professional, social, financial. You should know right now that one more motor vehicle violation and my license is suspended. I'm not proud of that." Jerry looks at me like I'm nuts, like maybe he doesn't want this kind of wacko in the club. Uh-oh.

"How about costs?" I ask. "Initiation fees, bonds, annual assessments?"

He hands me an application, a single xeroxed sheet that asks your name and address and to circle the kind of membership you want. My annual membership will be $325 plus a $50 credit voucher.

"Can *women* be full members?" Jody asks firmly.

"Only women with three seventy-five can," Jerry replies.

"How about monthly minimums?" she asks.

"Nope," Jerry replies.

"That's all if—*if*—we're accepted," I say, waiting for him to drop the big one about the ten-year waiting list or the blackball system.

"Your chances are good," Jerry remarks, "since we've never turned anyone down." He said if we filled in our names and address and wrote him a check, we were in. Jody and I looked at each other. Too easy. We told him we'd take the form home and think about it.

"Of course you have to abide by all the rules," Jerry reminds us. This *is* a country club, but the rules here don't come in bound volumes. They all fit neatly on a sign by the first tee:

"Shirt and Shoes Required" (Same as McDonald's, but *why both?*).

"Every Golfer Must Have Golf Clubs" (Although you might get away with garden implements or hockey sticks).

No coolers (Buy our beer or drink yours hot).

Ten-stroke limit per hole (Fine—helps my score).

Slower Players Let Faster Players Play Through ("Faster players" are those who've been removing the governors from the golf carts and speeding down fairways at forty miles per hour).

Carts are to be operated in safe manner and are to remain on golf course at all times (Golfers often drive carts on city streets to nearby West Side Market to purchase ice and beer for illicit coolers).

As president and chief law enforcement officer for Goat Hill, Jerry says it is sometimes necessary to enforce the rules when people try to play bare-chested or barefoot. And although they've never turned anyone down for membership, they did kick one member out of the club for getting drunk all the time and screaming ethnic jokes that were not only offensive but, moreover, not funny enough.

Jerry says they have to maintain some sense of decorum: "People get married here."

12

The City Game

I meant to take up golf twenty years ago. But we moved to New York and I couldn't figure out where to play. You can't join a nice private club like Diane and Rick's when you're knocking down thirty-seven-five as a newspaper reporter, and the city's public golf courses were . . . different.

We discovered that in golf, as in life, *everything* was a little different in New York. Take golf course hazards, for example, which tend to be of the sand and water varieties elsewhere, but which were far more diverse on New York City's public courses.

Out on the Pelham Golf Course in the Bronx, Don Jerome told me that one of his tee shots had recently bounced into an abandoned car on the fairway, costing him a stroke. He said that on another occasion, a friend of his was robbed while lining up an approach shot, costing him no strokes, but $65 and his credit cards. "Something like that will disrupt a golfer's concentration," Don noted.

"I know a guy who used to take his dog golfing with him for protection," said another golfer, James McDonald. He recalled that someone else carried a can of Mace in his bag alongside his woods and irons.

"It would really be smarter to play in eightsomes or sixteensomes," added Charlie Pessoni.

Back then these guerrilla golfers blamed the city's fiscal crisis and crime wave for all this and said conditions had been improving under a new program in which the city licensed private companies to operate its courses.

"We are in a mild state of shock," admitted Kimble Knowlden, who had recently come to the city to oversee the improvement and operation of the public courses for the American Golf Corporation of Los Angeles.

"You have to remember that we're from California," said Kimble, once the head golf pro at Pebble Beach, which of course is one of the world's grandest courses.

"Here," he said, "there were assaults and robberies right on the courses. If you left your car in the lot while you played, it would probably be gone when you returned. Graffiti was all over everything. The well water at a course on Staten Island was so polluted that when you used it to water the course all the grass turned black. And people were using the courses as trash dumps."

"Tell him about the bodies, Kimble," said John DeMatteo, another American Golf supervisor. "We get a certain number of dead bodies deposited on the courses. I try not to be the first one out on the course in the morning."

"At the Dyker Beach course in Brooklyn," John said, "it was lovely in the morning, mowing the tall grass and watching the rats hop here and there like bunnies." He said area residents complained about the golf course clean-ups because it destroyed the habitats of the rats, which then sought refuge in nearby homes.

Things began to improve, and more golfers were returning, but many problems peculiar to the city game persisted. Youths still ran out of the bushes and stole golf carts while the drivers were putting. The manager of the Clearview course spent a good deal of time roaming the streets of Queens retrieving his carts and driving them back to the course on expressways.

"Abandoned automobiles on the course are a perpetual problem," Kimble acknowledged. "Auto thieves love to drive them onto the courses where they get stuck in the sand traps."

At first he employed armed security guards at the courses. But as crime diminished and in the interest of providing a "country-club atmosphere," he replaced the uniformed guards with a force of unarmed "marshals" made up largely of retired men who liked to play golf. They patrolled the course looking for people trying to sneak on without paying—an offense common to even the most exclusive suburban clubs—and the marshals reported felonies in progress to the NYPD. They also did away with high-security cashier cages, which were most un-country-club-like.

"New Yorkers love to beat the system," he said. "We catch people sneaking on the course and they say 'so try to stop me.' " We call the cops and they say 'What!? Are you kidding? We've got three murders over here we're working on.' "

With so few open spaces in the city, the golf courses are used as soccer fields, picnic areas, dirt-bike courses, lovers lanes, and what have you. "They usually get out of the way," said Jane Angelo, one of the many women golfers beginning to reappear on public courses after things became a bit safer. "They stopped what appeared to be a gang fight once to let us play through."

"We try to live and let live now," Kimble said, adding that a number of people had taken up residence in tents on golf course property and were allowed to stay so long as they were out of bounds.

He said that when American Golf took over it had to hire "ex-cops or large firemen" as starters—bouncers really—at the courses, because of the terrible arguments over whose turn it was to play.

"Before they took over," said Lou Avon, who had played a Bronx course for twenty years, "we had to come here at 1:00 A.M. to get in line to play. That in itself makes people irritable. Now, they have a phone reservation system, and there aren't as many fistfights. It is becoming a country club for the average man."

Things have improved dramatically. Where once there were rats on the Pelham and Split Rock courses, now there are foxes, rabbits, and colorful birds, including pheasants, quail, and a mother duck hatching some eggs fifty yards from Pelham's 7th hole.

And out in the nearly-filled-to-capacity parking lot that was once an abandoned weed field, one can observe expensive cars, including a Mercedes convertible with "MD" license plates.

*   *   *

You can play golf anywhere these days, even in Manhattan. The elevator is on the right. After pulling off the West Side Highway, the rumble and roar of its heavy traffic punctuated by jackhammers, one passes through the portal of a vast, old, enclosed pier to encounter what appears to be an urban mirage: the clapboard facade of . . . a country club? Yes, with a putting green right outside the front door, and valet parking if you like.

No sight is left unseen in New York. But here's a new one for the books: two guys with full sets of golf clubs riding New York's 23rd Street bus, in January.

They could be headed to a mental health facility, or they could be headed here, to the Chelsea Piers Golf Club, complete with the putting green, a golf academy, sixteen golf pros, a pro shop, a sand trap, and a driving range. It is a complete golf club right in Manhattan—except, of course, for the rather conspicuous absence of a golf course, an amenity people have come to expect when they join a golf club. But there is a vast bar, which of course runs a close second to golf in terms of importance. The club offers memberships, camps, even golf stretching clinics.

After 5:00 P.M. and all day on weekends the place is packed. Molly Lonigan, a twenty-eight-year-old Wall Streeter, says she is probably going to join the club, which will cost her $1,000, but will give her discounts, a locker, storage for her golf bag, and guaranteed tee times, among other things.

She likes golf and thinks taking it up will be good for business. "We're invited to a lot of these corporate golf outings," she says.

Her friend Deborah says she is trying to play golf, but isn't really all that keen on the game.

"I just want to meet men," Deborah admits. "Seriously. Rich men."

"So do I," says their friend Jim.

Okay, then.

The Golf Club is but a small part of this $100 million, 1.7 million square foot sports complex, fashioned from once grand piers that had of late been reduced to a site for garbage truck repairs, as well as the single most hostile spot in all of New York (and that's saying something): the pound where spitting-mad motorists came to retrieve their towed vehicles, after discussing the matter with city employees hiding behind bulletproof glass and reinforced steel counters.

The indoor sports complex now comprises two ice rinks, two in-line skating rinks, basketball courts, soccer fields, batting cages, a gymnastics center, a health club, beach volleyball court, fifty-five-foot climbing wall, forty-lane bowling alley, boxing ring, spa, the world's longest indoor running track, swimming pool, sporting goods stores, marina, restaurants, and a brew pub—as well as a fashion photo studio, and TV and movie studios.

But I find the driving range to be the wonder of it all: fifty-two heated, weather-protected stalls on four levels, from where dozens of balls are flying at any one time, out toward the Hudson River, and Hoboken beyond. Nets sixteen stories high and two hundred yards downrange at the end of the pier stop the balls before they land in the river or New Jersey. The nets also enclose the sides of the range, protecting big yachts docked here by the likes of Steve Forbes and Geraldo Rivera.

The range is completely automated. Completely. "You never touch your balls," boasts the guy at the front desk. Which, come to think of it, might be something they'd want to enscript in Latin on the Chelsea Piers Golf Club crest, no?

It's all very Japanese. You see gargantuan net structures like this every couple of minutes as you travel along the highways in Tokyo. The Japanese are even crazier about golf than we are, if that's possible, and land is at a premium. You've probably heard tales of their multimillion-dollar golf club memberships, not to mention the golf religion with a driving range atop the temple. It was a Japanese team that installed these nets here at Chelsea Piers, as well as the completely automated ball system that vacuums up the balls on the course, shoots them through tubes upstairs, completely bypassing any need for buckets, and automatically places them on the tees, one after another, so that you never touch your balls.

Tu Numquam Tactus Tuum Globi.

My wife complained at another driving range about having to bend down to tee up a hundred balls, and how the next day her legs hurt. Well, here you don't have to bend down. The range is equipped with Japanese auto-teeing devices, called CompuTees. You swipe your credit or debit card through the machine at each tee, and you receive anywhere from 65 balls for $15 during peak hours, up to 625 balls for $100 off-peak, and unlimited balls from 5:00 A.M. to 8:00 A.M. for $20. CompuTee gives you your current RPB (Rate Per Ball) on digital readout. It also gives you your tee height in millimeters, and tee height adjustment capability. You can rent a club for $4.

Five A.M.? Golfers are addicts who will rise at any hour to feed their habit. And, New Yorkers tend to have type A personalities to boot. The range is open from 5:00 A.M. to midnight.

Six hundred twenty-five balls for a hundred bucks? Does *anyone* ever hit six hundred twenty-five balls?

"Oh yes," says William, the manager, "one lady has come and hit a thousand."

A thousand?

"Yes, more than once."

Was she a good golfer?

"No."

Did she appear angry?

"No."

Disturbed? Possessed?

William says he's no psychiatrist, but then: Who that plays golf is not possessed?

I come on my lunch hour. You take an elevator to play golf! A sign inside the elevator reminds me that no drivers or woods are allowed on the fourth floor of the driving range, because balls have been hit over the top of the net, striking vessels on the Hudson. This is the kind of childish thing I would do on purpose—if only I could hit it that far. As it is, I have to content myself with trying to hit the guy driving the golf ball sweeper.

I take the elevator to the fourth floor and love it up there. I notice my drives go farther when I hit them from forty feet in the air. Not straighter, just farther.

Also, there are guys up here Worse Than I Am. Honestly. I just wish I'd asked their names. They are Wall Street brokers who say "the market's so damned bad we're playing golf instead"—at one o'clock on a weekday afternoon. This frightens me. If their golf is better than the market this day, then the crash of '29 was but a mild dip, a little correction, and thousands of people must be jumping out of skyscrapers right now. After seeing them hit the ball, I am surprised, frankly, that these men are not leaping from the tees here on the fourth floor out of total humiliation. Japanese men would. All you have to do is take three steps forward.

One of them *looks* absolutely *marvelous*. He's dressed all in black, from his cashmere golf shirt, alligator belt, plush trousers, and socks, down to his black alligator golf shoes. An estimated $800 outfit I would say, even if he said he lived in New Jersey to avoid the 8 1/2 percent sales tax (although that is not enough to make some people say they live in New Jersey). His driver is, of course, very large and mostly titanium.

He even looks good addressing the ball, and his swing doesn't even look that bad to me, although with my knowledge of the game, Little Stevie Wonder could size up his swing just as well.

But his drives were just . . . awful. Horrible, 45 degree slices, and 45 degree hooks. It was downright Pythagorean.

But his partner is the one I really want to tell you about, a lanky guy with a new set of custom Callaway clubs that he'd just received yesterday at a cost of $3,000 (plus $500 for the shoes and bag).

On his first swing—ever—with his Great Big Bertha driver, he hit on his backswing one of the steel trusses that hold the place up. Thick, strong steel girders riveted in place in 1910. Strong enough that when the *Queen Elizabeth* docked here, the girders wouldn't move. His swing was one of the worst moments here at Pier 59 since the *Titanic* failed to show up as scheduled in April of 1912.

You've heard of Ping clubs? Well this was a CLANG! Everyone stopped to look. He should have leaped off the fourth floor tee—hari-kari-style—but did not. Miraculously, the club and the pier appeared to be okay and he continued. Brad, who works here, says he has seen balls ricochet off the pier superstructure but this is the first time he's ever seen a golfer hit the pier with a club. Brad suggests we preventatively move away to a safer distance.

On the pier-whacker's second swing—ever—with his new driver, which he said cost more than $500, he did not hit the pier, which was good. He hit the Astroturf behind his ball with an emphatic THUD! before the club struck the ball.

Not a bad hit, though. Not bad at all. I see it sailing off toward the Garden State.

But wait! That's not the ball in flight . . . it's Great Big Bertha's humongous head! The head was recovered by a rescue team more than a hundred yards downrange, which I thought was pretty darned good distance.

This made me feel good, sort of like when a soldier in combat sees someone else shot and is secretly glad inside it's not him. I'm not proud of this.

But it was a reminder: No matter how bad you are, somebody's always worse.

I went downstairs and wandered through the Greg Norman pro shop. I wasn't ready for any of that stuff. Not ready for the expensive Taylor Innergel balls, and definitely not ready for the Greg Norman hat. I'd look like . . . me . . . wearing the World Wrestling Federation title belt.

When I returned my rented club with the head still on, I was feeling very good about my game.

I told the guy who'd lost his head that I was just taking up golf.

"I have a word of advice for you," he replied. "Don't."

13

SwingCam: Golf in the 21st Century

Maybe advanced computer technology can help. I'd seen the SwingCam Advanced Visual Learning System at the PGA Golf Merchandise Show and here it was again at Chelsea Piers.

"This is the twenty-first century," a sales rep at the Golf Show notified us. "Time to bring computer technology to your golf game. Could take off half a dozen strokes." (That's minus 68 now, and counting!)

He generously offered Jody and me complimentary computer golf swing analyses, using his SwingCam Advanced Visual Learning System with Doppler radar. Wow! Doppler radar, just like the weathergal uses on NewsChannel 4! I worry, however, that it might show the fog and scattered showers in my armpits. Playing golf in front of others, not to mention before a video camera, makes me sweat.

But in desperate need of help, I agreed to swing at a ball

while a computer sat hunkered down across from me analyzing my every move. It did not laugh when I swung (as others do), or even say anything, it just professionally recorded my swing with a video camera and left the talking to a golf scientist person who interpreted the results using Advanced Planar Analysis.

"We can see on the digital readout that you drove the ball ninety yards," the expert pointed out to me. Not good. He told me my clubhead speed was slow, as was my ball speed, and noted that my front foot moved a lot and my head went up way too soon. None of it good.

"Do people ever just *slap* you?" I asked.

"We try to be as positive as we can and still be helpful," he replied.

The IRU (Instant Replay Unit) digitally captured my golf swing and had the temerity to show it to me in slo-mo and freeze frames. It wasn't pretty.

The golf scientist said the Main Kiosk Unit was linked to the IRU and could provide my body sway measurements as well as my swing plane. But I figured I'd had enough bad news for one day and besides, I had no idea what he was even *talking* about. The unit could also provide a side-by-side (unfavorable) comparison of a golf pro's swing with my own. No thanks.

He said my swing was now on their Internet Web site and could be downloaded at any time by a golf pro for further study. I told him that would be tantamount to calling in the curator of the Metropolitan Museum of Art to analyze my kids' finger painting.

He said I can "cyber-rent tools" to fix my golf swing, but I am afraid I would cyber-forget to return them and have to pay virtual late fees. He informed us that tips and suggested drills can also be provided "to develop and reinforce the latest in biomechanic training."

At which point my wife informed *him* that she objected to the low camera angle employed by the SwingCam Advanced Visual Learning System with Doppler radar, which she felt made her ass look big.

I again encounter SwingCam out in the real world here at Chelsea Piers, where one of the tees is SwingCam-equipped. It looks something like an ATM sitting there, except you pay it, not the other way around.

You put in your credit card, it charges you $9.95, and for the next ten minutes that same damned machine sitting on the other side of the tee records your swings and plays them back in slow motion for you on a monitor. Talk about bad TV! Although, really, how many sitcoms are *this* funny?

Two terrible golfers are using the tee equipped with SwingCam, even though they are not using the Swing-Cam itself, and even though furthermore it's a rainy, cold weekday at two in the afternoon and most of the other fifty-two tees are wide open. What they are doing is *hiding* behind the SwingCam machine—an unintended, but fair, use. When your golf swing's as grotesque as theirs, you *should* hide yourself from public view. They are the golfing equivalents of the Elephant Man.

When they finish, I step up to SwingCam and the first thing I notice is that there's a large chunk out of the machine, either from an errant swing that would warrant the help offered by this advanced visual learning system, or from a golfer pissed off at the machine for what it's telling the customer about his or her game.

I swipe my card and have to decide which of the three unlabeled buttons to press—kind of like a shell game. Unfortunately, I choose a button that turns the machine off. I swipe my card again, hit another unlabeled button and this time get lucky. I do a lot of swiping before it's over and will not be surprised to find several $9.95s on my Amex bill totaling around $200.

This SwingCam also videotapes your swing, plays it back, and provides digital readout of the distance you hit the ball, club speed, and ball speed.

My first set of readings are absolutely phenomenal, representing my finest hour in golf!

Distance: 288 yards!

Club speed: 92 miles per hour!

Ball speed: 162 miles per hour!

I love this machine.

These are great stats! But they are not *my* stats. Maybe the last guy's. SwingCam is on the fritz. It read 288 yards, yet I had actually *seen* my drive hit just beyond the second "green" on the range, which is eighty-seven yards away. So, there seemed to be this two-hundred-yard discrepancy. Unfortunately, I'd forgotten in my excitement to ask for a printout of those first stats to preserve in the family Bible.

I hit my second drive and SwingCam came to its senses.

Distance: 97 yards.

Club speed: 17 miles per hour.

Ball speed: 98 miles per hour.

Now these . . . these would be my statistics. Although I chose not to believe those either, charging that this . . . this . . . cheap vending machine . . . had lost all credibility.

I saved that drive in the SwingCam computer as my "Typical" swing, and another one, when the ball went a little farther, as my "Best" swing. SwingCam stores two of your swings for review on your home computer or the Main Kiosk in the lobby. Instructions say you may call up your swing on the screen and analyze it for Sway, Alignment, and Plane, as well as putting it on a split screen and comparing it with that of a golf pro on the other side of the screen.

I put my credit card into the Main Kiosk and up pops an image of me swinging. I start to analyze the swing—"ugly" would be a fair analysis of what I'm seeing—when I realize: It's not me! His hair is the same color, his build's the same, he's bent over so you can't see his face, and he's pretty bad. But those aren't my shoes. That isn't my shirt. He's indoors somewhere. This is the World Wide Web. Whoever this is may be practicing in his basement in Rangoon. It's not me.

I ask a man walking by—a golf pro, or assistant pro, or perhaps the man who fills the candy machine—to assist me. He agrees it's Not Me. We go back to SwingCam and do it all over again, except this time he presses the unlabeled buttons, and with greater success. Returning to the Main Kiosk, we do manage to call up Me swinging on the screen. It's not a pretty thing to watch. For some reason that Rangoon guy appears, too, right beside me. It looks like a bad vaudeville act.

"Maybe he's the pro," says the guy helping me. Then we

watch him swing and realize that if he's the pro I'm Nancy Lopez.

My helper presses a button that produces two lines down the screen, one on either side of my body, so we can analyze my Sway. Now here is another place where this system breaks down. The SwingCam sign upstairs says "See Your Swing, Analyze Your Swing, Download Your Swing—By Yourself!"

This is like someone inventing TumorCam, which for $9.95 gives you an X ray of your brain tumor that you can See, Download, and Cure—Yourself!

For openers: What *is* this . . . Sway? Apparently, it is not good. Do I have it? Is it terminal? Or, do I need more . . . Sway? What if I'm suffering from Sway Deficiency Anemia and don't know it?

"I don't think you have much Sway," says my helper, who then adds that he's "not really a golfer" himself.

"So, what do you recommend from the candy machine?" I ask.

"What?" he replies.

"Nothing," I say.

He says he's no expert, he's just watched others try to use SwingCam, that's all. He hits another button that draws a circle around my head and we put our two heads together and come up with the conclusion that my head: (a) is too big, since the circle won't even go around it; and (b) probably moves too much and looks up too soon.

He hits the Alignment button and I appear to be out of alignment. I'm starting to feel like an '84 Volare at a Sears Car Care Diagnostic Center. The Plane button makes two red spears appear but to what end we aren't at all sure.

So, without someone practiced telling me how to work SwingCam, and without a pro to analyze my problems and knowledgeably utilize the tools of analysis, SwingCam is of little help to me the novice golfer.

How about just forgetting the damned technology and asking one of the sixteen pros here to watch me swing for ten minutes and to recommend adjustments—or perhaps another sport here at the pier?

Another aspect of SwingCam is that you can download those two swings from your home computer and study them or even send them to a pro for cyber-analysis. I do this. My swing is on the World Wide Web for all the world to see! How embarrassing. Given the option, I'd have opted for a Web cam in my bathroom.

With my awful images on the screen I try to hire a golf pro to analyze my swing, but can't seem to do it. I call the SwingCam offices and they say they haven't quite hired the pros yet. I say they probably can't find one to take my case.

I pressed another button for the free golf lesson offered by the Internet Golf Academy. Here a student named Bill (Not Me) had his swing analyzed amidst a flurry of critiques from a pro regarding his "overall ball flight pattern," "shaft plane," "shoulder plane," "power drains," "arm collapse," "impact position," his bad 104 degree arm angle, and the need to "reroute" his backspin. So much to think about! No kid could ever hit a baseball, sink a jump shot, kick a soccer ball with this much crap running through his head. Are you absolutely sure this is a sport?

A month went by and I decided to see if SwingCam had any golf pros lined up yet. I put in my locator number to access my golf swings on the computer and there on the screen was a handsome black man in a white shirt swinging a golf club. Again: Not Me.

SwingCam, like everything else I tried, seemed unable to help with my golf game.

14

Goat Hill Golf

I *could* win today. I'm playing golf with my wife, Jody, and she's never even *played* the game before.

Although we still haven't decided to join yet, we're golfing at Goat Hill, an ideal setting for us. It's certainly one of the least humiliating, a course that's not all that challenging and, as mentioned, casual in the extreme. I've seen golfers here in blue jean cutoffs and sleeveless black Metallica T-shirts, swigging beer while watching a partner putt with a cigarette in his mouth. The guy was good, too.

On the way we stop at Grandpa (Jerry) Brennan's Previously Owned Golf Ball Emporium across the street. Should we get colored balls? They might be easier to find. But possibly embarrassing. We decide to buy in bulk, figuring we'll need as many as we can carry. The cheapest are five for a dollar. They come in sandwich bags, which could also be embarrassing. We buy twenty-five balls and pray that's enough.

It isn't. I do believe I set my personal record for lost balls that day, more than a dozen surrendered to the lush growth of this rainy summer. By hole 7, in fact, they were completely gone. On 8 I scoured the depths of my bag and came up with a Dunkin' Donuts logo ball, followed by a few XXXX-out balls, another ball that seemed to have three distinct sides, and finally a ball that appeared to have been backed over by a car. On the final hole, Jody took her ball out of the cup and said "feel this." It was some sort of soft rubber, a Maxfli that felt as though it had been poached.

There never seems to be any waiting at Goat Hill, you just pay up at the bar—$36.99 for the two of us and the cart—and have at it. Although some of these guys dressed to mow the lawn are surprisingly good golfers, the overall level of play here is comforting to me. On the first tee a man is swinging very hard and wild, as if trying to bust a piñata. As if blindfolded, he is missing.

The first concern here is that the golf cart parking area is twenty feet in *front* of (if somewhat lower than) the first tee. I miss them, this time, my opening drive slicing high to the right, clear over the nets meant to protect the dirt road leading up to the club, and bouncing in front of an advancing pickup truck. I make an adjustment, and hook my next shot into a stand of trees to the left. So, my first two swings result in two lost balls.

On her first hole ever, Jody is doing better than I, tenaciously hacking her way toward the green. At the first green there is earthmoving equipment doing some heavy

147

landscaping—*while* we play. And to think the pros object to camera clicks. And, alas, our putting game, once the strength of the Geist family golf dynasty (owing to all the hours of mini-golf we've put in) has deserted us.

On hole 2, we did *not* hit Jerry Brennan's golf ball stand or his house, which are just across the road from the fairway. That was sort of disappointing—although I did hit the road. My friend Robert once hit a biker on the road with his drive from that second tee. Dropped him in his tire tracks. Robert isn't so good either. He plays in the morning at Goat Hill before the course opens so no one will see him.

Jerry is out in his yard watching us, just as Jody takes a big swing at the ball, misses, and does a pirouette.

"Want me to play some ballet music?" he yells from across the road. Now I know why the PGA doesn't hold tournaments here. One reason why.

She's having trouble making contact, hitting either over the ball or behind it. I am having no trouble hitting the ball, but direction is a problem. But she does finally connect, and sends her ball slicing across the two-lane highway. Gamely, she decides to play it as it lays. Traffic slows apprehensively at the sight of this crazed golfer preparing to hit a ball lying in the rough a foot from the side of the road. (Later at the bar, a fellow duffer will helpfully suggest she carry orange traffic cones in her golf bag to stop traffic.) She waits until the traffic passes in the far lane, holds up traffic in the near lane by putting up her left hand, then swats the ball—nicely, I must say—back onto the fairway. I'm proud of her determination. It reminded me of the woman who once hit a ball into a creek, chased it in a rowboat, and whacked it back upstream to take a 166 on the hole.

On the third tee, I hooked one into a tree, a shot that ricocheted back by the ladies' tee. Jody hit the steel mesh garbage can positioned there. We were getting pretty good at hitting our bad shots close together, synchronized golf, which is convenient, makes for speedy play, and like synchronized swimming, is beautiful to watch.

As we drive off in the cart, her clubs fall off the back. Neither of us has had any experience strapping golf bags to carts. This is the place to learn. Later a golfer will give us back a 3-wood we didn't pick up there at the accident scene. The club was so old and beat-up I almost denied it was ours.

Next, Jody hits an exceptional shot almost in the hole, only to watch a little girl bound onto the green and retrieve it. "Hey, you little shit," we yell, and make her put it back. She is with her father, who probably brings her golfing to snatch as many golf balls as she can. Who, but us, would yell at a cute little girl?

The next hole is odd. It's one where you hit a tee shot straight up a steep hill and watch it roll back down, time after time. The green is down at the bottom of the other side of the hill and you clang a big dinner bell to let players behind you know when you've finished. The reason the course is called Goat Hill, one historian at the bar says, "is that you gotta be dumber than goat shit to walk up and down these hills."

Then come a couple of holes we'd both rather forget, and in fact have. I just remember the final hole on this 9-hole course, because people sit on the clubhouse porch, right behind the last green, behind very heavy screens, and watch.

When my son Willie and I play here, after 8 holes, 60 strokes, and twenty-five lost balls, he begins a mock television broadcast as we walk up the 9th fairway that's worthy of a smarmy network broadcast of the Masters in Augusta: "Now, in the golden late-afternoon sunlight these two champions make the historic walk up the august 9th fairway here at venerable Goat Hill, as Snead, Palmer, and Nicklaus have done before them . . . the dry, brown fairways swirling with dust, the bittersweet vines strangling the life out of the trees, the fawns frantically dodging mis-hit golf balls . . ."

The 9th green is elevated, like a ten-foot-high stage on which putters perform for the entertainment of those on the porch just fifteen feet away. We always give them a good show. I chip nicely to the green and begin putting, and putting, and putting. I'm feeling the pressure of the audience. My final three-foot putt stops short of the cup and I hit it again on my follow-through, counting the whole thing as just one stroke.

"Where's the scorecard?" I ask.

"Threw it out a long time ago," Jody says.

"Good," I say. "Make sure you always tear them up in little pieces like you do with credit card receipts. Don't want something like that lying around."

Later we sit on that porch going over our games. I figure I had the one legitimate bogey, several near legitimate 6s, and some higher scores I'd rather not mention. I figured my score was about an illegitimate 60 for 9 holes— legitimately probably nearer 70. Not good, considering this is a thoroughly unchallenging course with almost no hazards. I'm not even sure who won. We figure if we put all of our best shots together we would have maybe parred one hole. I think I was dehydrated though, my electrolytes a little low.

Once when Willie and I finished here he said: "It was horrible, but I'm glad we did it."

What an odd thing to say, but no more so than my response: "Me, too." Golf can be really strange that way. It must be the camaraderie and the togetherness, like if the two of us had just changed a flat tire together.

When Jody and I turned in our cart key, the bartender asked how we'd done and we admitted: not very well.

"But, I'll bet you two had fun," he laughs.

"No," I mutter, "not really." Not at all.

15

There's the Fairway and Then There's My Way

Help me out a little. The Rules of Golf, as set forth by the United States Golf Association and the Royal and Ancient Golf Club of St. Andrews, Scotland, are voluminous, read like federal statutes, take all the fun out of the game, and have basically been formulated to restrict the best golfers.

But what about us? So-called bad golfers represent the vast majority and need alleviation from this veritable strangulation by draconian regulations and restrictive covenants. Herewith, then, a few simple rules changes to aid beginners and others suffering with high handicaps who are going to just damned *quit* if we don't get some relief:

1. Play the closest hole. Player may at any time elect to play the closest hole regardless of numerical designation.

2. Since this is not billiards, player need not "call" the intended hole in advance.

3. If opening drive from first tee lands on or near the 9th or 18th green (usually situated near the first tee and the clubhouse), golfer may opt (under Rule No. 1) to play the 9th or 18th and *quit*.

> 3a. That single hole score, however, shall not be represented as a score for a complete round of 9 or 18 holes unless greater than par for the entire course.

4. Player need not play 9 or 18 distinctly *different* holes.

5. Player keeps own score, if at all.

6. Out-of-bounds-my-ass. There is no out of bounds—a concept for prissy unadventuresome sorts fearful of wilderness treks and crossing highways.

7. When hitting out of a private home or condominium, every effort should be made to hit ball back out of the same broken window ball entered.

> 7a. If lie is in shag carpeting, ball may be placed on a flat surface such as a coffee table.

8. If ball is hit into "soft foods" such as shrimp, egg, or potato salads, or tiramisu, in dining room or outside "patio" dining areas, the foodstuffs may be eaten away from ball's surface to diminish splatter when player hits out. Balls on "hard foods," such as day-old kaiser rolls, however, must be played as they lie.

9. Balls hit into club swimming pool may be moved to shallow end and played.

10. Balls felling other golfers shall not be played off downed individuals per se.

10a. Victims may be moved if they present an obstruction, but original position should be outlined in chalk.

11. Golfers playing balls from across adjacent roadways may employ cones or other traffic control devices.

12. Gimmee putts are encouraged.

12a. Gimmees become longer on later holes, e.g., one foot on 1st hole, eighteen feet on 18th.

12b. Entire gimmee *holes* may be taken, with a "fair" score recorded for the hole, such as a 2.

12c. All fourth putts for triple bogeys are gimmees.

13. Mulligans, yes, always.

13a. If mulligan is somehow worse than original shot, then a third "mcmulligan" is to be taken, and best of three played.

14. "Tae Kwon Do Golf" rules in effect—with use of hands and feet allowed.

14a. Tosses, throws, and kicks are not sanctioned by USGA rules, and are therefore technically not strokes and need not be counted.

15. Golfers may not urinate within two club lengths of cart path.

16. Whiffs are practice swings (so long as player does not indicate that he or she missed by mistake).

17. Balls hit less than ten feet are not deemed officially "hit" balls and are not to be counted.

18. Player may rehit without penalty if there was a distracting noise (e.g., bird chirp)—even if noise emanated from player (e.g., belch or the breaking of wind).

19. "Forward Progress" rule is in effect. Balls rolling backward or ricocheting back from rocks, trees, carts, cars,

homes, etc., are placed at closest point to hole achieved.

20. "Invisible Gallery" rule. Pros use galleries as human backstops, so any ball we hit more than five feet into the rough or more than ten feet past a green (where pro galleries stand) is to be placed where it would have been stopped if we, too, had galleries.

21. If playing on another fairway, in the woods, or otherwise out of sight of others in your party, let conscience be your guide.

22. Follow rules of Eco-Golf. Smashing down or standing on bushes to improve your shot encourages spring growth; same with pruning extraneous tree limbs; and as for clearing weeds, well, that's practically like performing community service.

23. However, should taking a difficult shot potentially endanger wildlife, plants, wetlands, or sandy "beach" areas, ball should be moved to a less ecologically fragile area—like mid-fairway.

24. "Double Jeopardy" rule. This is America and no golfer can be cruelly repunished for misplay on the same hole, e.g., if you hit your ball from one bunker to another you get to take it out. No penalty.

16
What's Your Handicap?

Okay, so I can't beat really mediocre men or little, middle-aged women or seemingly anybody really. But, maybe I could beat someone who's totally *blind*.

I read an astonishing newspaper article on blind golfers—What?—that went on to tell of a big Blind Golf Association tournament scheduled nearby. Sure. And next week there's a blind NASCAR drivers race. C'mon. This *had* to be a joke, probably a hoax some prankster concocted and sent to a clueless newspaper editor.

Yet, when I called the country club where the tourney was supposedly taking place, instead of laughing, they confirmed it. Elaborate hoax.

Being the naturally competitive type, unafraid of any challenge life throws at me, I tossed my (wife's) clubs in the car, and raced over. But, wait! Should I take a cane? Stop by and pick up my friend's dog? I found some sunglasses in the glove compartment and slipped them on.

Pulling into the Mt. Kisco Country Club, I had no idea what to expect, really, maybe a bunch of goof-offs in blindfolds having their idea of a wacky golf outing. I did give the other cars wide berth, however, just in case these were truly blind golfers driving in for the tournament.

What I found was unbelievable, an announcer heralding the opening of the annual Ken Venturi Guiding Eyes Golf Classic featuring sixteen of the world's best *blind golfers!* (Fifteen of these male oxymorons and one woman.) The announcer didn't seem to be kidding, either.

But . . . how could this possibly *be?*

The gallery intently observed as the first golfer, Keith Melick, who the announcer said had won the previous two of these Corcoran Cup competitions, stepped to the tee. Each golfer has a coach, in this case Keith's wife, Jean, who points him in precisely the right direction and helps adjust his stance and his distance from the ball. The coach also gives the golfer the same information any caddie might, such as distance to the green, positions of hazards, and so forth. Some coaches crouch and place the clubhead directly behind the ball. And, when everything is perfectly aligned, the coach gives a "yep," or a word to that effect, and the golfer swings.

Let the clichés fall where they may, I watched in absolute stunned disbelief as Keith's opening drive took off like a shot, straight and true, two hundred yards down the fairway. I don't know what I expected, but not *this!* Was he, you know, *peeking?* The gallery applauded.

David Meador, Keith's partner at this "Masters of Blind Golf" classic, stepped up and did the same thing! So did the next guy, Pat Browne, who had a 1 handicap before going blind and who's won this tournament seventeen times. At this point, it wouldn't have surprised me to see them jump in their carts and drive off.

I finally came to my senses, and tagged along with the fourth twosome, Andy Stewart from Alabama and Ron Tomlinson from England. (They had a little trouble understanding each other at first.) Andy, thirty-three, suddenly—in the course of just forty-eight hours—went completely blind nine years ago from a neuropathic disease. He was operating at even more of a disadvantage this day, having suffered spinal injuries from swinging his golf clubs too hard, and now walking around with two rods, two plates, and eight screws in his back. Other than that (and a torn ligament), he was perfectly fine. "I can't complain," he said with a smile. I almost broke into tears when he said that, and might have, except the guy plays golf better than I do.

Andy routinely drove the ball well over two hundred yards. And, oh yeah, straight. He'd hit the ball, then ask where it went. I told him that I do the very same thing. It just doesn't take him as long to find his. He doesn't slice it like I do, probably because he's not lifting his head up too soon—a common fault among slicers—to see where it went. He has certain advantages.

Andy says he's been playing golf for six years, having learned the game after he went blind, has driven a ball 265 yards, has scored an 83 for 18 holes and a 38 on a 9-hole course.

"Bull!" I say.

"There were witnesses," replied Andy's coach, his nephew David Witt.

In this tournament, they do play winter rules, which means they can roll a ball over if it's in a divot, but other than that it's all fair and square. They don't hit from the ladies' tees, nothing like that. And unlike my rules, whiffs count and there are no gimmees.

Andy won't have scores that good here. This is a tough course. Sometimes I think he's better off not being able to see some of the downright diabolical holes. Hole 6, for example, features a tiny green precariously perched atop a veritable beach of sand that surrounds it like a moat. Par-4. Andy bogeys the hole. The man can flat-out pitch.

"I really don't tell him about all the traps," David says. On hole 8, he doesn't tell him about the two TV news camera crews either. Too much pressure. He tells him after he's played the hole. Andy is chagrined because he hasn't played it well, but finally says: "Oh well, I don't watch much TV myself."

To judge distance, the golfers pace off their chip shots and putts. On one hole, David and Andy measure thirteen and a half paces, but David tells him to hit "about a five and a half or a five and three fourths" because of the downhill slope. Andy is on the green in 3, but 3-putts for a 6.

Andy blames David for misreading the green, just like any other golfer would blame a caddie or a helpful partner. He complains that the slow play of the twosome ahead of them is holding them up, just like other golfers. And he carries on constant banter like other golfers do: "Boy, Ron, you hit that one completely out of sight!"

At the end of 9 holes in the tournament, there is a cut. Andy makes it, but this time Ron does not. Surprisingly, neither does Bob Andrews, who's finished second here twice. Bob is president of the United States Blind Golf Association, which currently sports about a hundred members who must be totally blind and prove that they've shot at least a legitimate 125 for 18 holes on three occasions. (Were it not for the "blind" and "legitimate" parts, I could join.) He says there's a whole worldwide tour for blind golfers.

Figuring Bob is having an off day, and that he's totally blind, I challenge him to play a hole.

"What's your handicap?" I ask, "if you'll pardon the expression."

"Twenty-nine," he says, informing me that one blind golfer plays to a 14 or 15 handicap. (A blind golfer once shot a 77, and one of the golfers here has shot a hole-in-one!) He says some of his sighted friends won't play golf with him because they figure it's a lose-lose situation. "It sure is fun to beat them when they do," he says. Hmmm.

He tells me the tale of the legendary blind golfer Charley Boswell challenging Jack Nicklaus (some versions have it Arnold Palmer or Bob Hope) to a round. Nicklaus accepts the challenge, and Boswell tells Nicklaus to meet him at the first tee—at midnight.

Bob's wife, Tina, is his coach. They have three sons. Tina doesn't put his ball down for him, and doesn't adjust his club. "I'm not gonna spend my life bowing down before my husband," she says. In soft, one-word directions, she has him move up or back, away from or toward the ball, and tells him to open or close his stance and his clubface. "It's very much a team sport," Bob says.

Later, Tina and Bob have me try to coach, something that proves most difficult. I have him facing this way and that, his club practically upside down and backward. It's like telling my cat to be a Seeing Eye dog.

But how *do* these golfers do it?

"You don't really need to see the ball," Bob explains. "The pros tell every golfer that they're just learning a good mechanical swing, and that the ball just gets in the way of that." It's muscle memory to the nth degree.

Bob tees off. His drive is another miracle to behold, quite long, although it does fade a bit to the right and lands a foot inside the rough. "I pretty much know where it is," Bob says, "by the sound and the feel."

The truth is, I need Tina to help line *me* up properly, but she won't. This is competition. So, my tee shot chops off short and to the left, landing at the ladies' tee. Sure Bob's blind, but I have some excuses, too: We're playing with his clubs and I don't have on golf shoes and I have a lot of junk in my pants pockets and a slight hangover. Even?

Bob and Tina take the cart on up ahead and I decide that for my second shot, I really need to throw the ball about twenty yards to get it out of there, and I go ahead and do that, and rather effectively if I do say so myself.

My second shot (the throw is not technically a shot) is an iron that is somewhere between a shank and a slice, but in any event doesn't reach his opening drive and so it's Still My Turn. My fourth advancement of the ball is a hard kick from the rough to the fairway, followed by my third shot, which carries past his first shot and—finally!—it's his turn. He hits it thin, frankly, but it rolls very, very far.

Bob lost his sight and nearly his life stepping on a

booby trap in Vietnam. He never balked for a moment at the idea of taking up golf, a game he'd never played. "I've sailed and I was fairly good at Ping-Pong, too, because I had a great serve," he notes. "Same with tennis, but it was hell if the other guy returned it." You'd have to be very lucky and carry a very big racket.

My fourth shot is fabulous, for me, a 6-iron that goes well over a hundred yards, and bounces on the green. Okay, it bounces off the other side of the green, too, but this ain't the friggin' Masters, now is it?

Maybe I *can* beat a blind golfer. Maybe I can. I would pray for victory but that would be wrong. Very wrong. Like, "Author–Bad Golfer Struck By Lightning"—that kind of wrong.

Bob's third shot is a perfectly executed bump and run that lands on the green about twenty feet from the hole. At this point, I start watching closely for signs that Bob can actually see. "Hey Bob!" I yell, pointing to the sky. "Look at that!" But he doesn't look. Shrewd guy.

I hit an 8-iron from some high grass five feet off the green, clear across the green to five feet on the other side. A nice shot, I figure, having improved my lie to shorter grass. I next hit onto the green and then begin my long-term putting project: one, two, three putts—for an 8 (not counting the toss and the kick).

Meanwhile, Bob, allegedly blind, is putting for par!

Tina hasn't told him a thing about the break of the green. Didn't tell me anything either. "I read the greens with my feet," he says, "by walking across them."

Word comes that Keith Melick has won the tournament for a third straight year with a score of 113—a bit disappointing to him because he shot a 103 here last year.

Tina pulls a blindfold from the golf bag and has me put it on. I see nothing, complete darkness, and my thoughts darken. How do people live like this, let alone play golf? They're so skillful you forget how disabled they really are. I am totally disoriented, of course, and off-balance. Tina lines me up with a ball she's dropped. I bend my knees, but then don't know how far I am from the ground. I get some sort of reading by touching my club to the ground, but it's not precise enough. I take a quarter swing and hit behind the ball, then hit it on top. It seems impossible.

Is there satisfaction to playing golf when you can't see the green grass and the beautiful flight of a well-struck ball?

"Absolutely," says Bob. "You're out with great people, you feel the sun, smell the grass and the fresh air, and hear and feel those great shots." And he doesn't have to watch the ugly ones.

After ten minutes of flailing at golf balls, I'm frustrated, I've had enough. I remove the blindfold. And see Bob. My heart sinks. How quickly and easily my precious sight has completely returned, just by ripping off the blindfold.

He misses his twenty-foot putt, as golfers do, leaving himself with a tap-in for a 5, on this par-4 hole. I had an illegitimate 8, but he didn't have those shadows on the green bothering him when he was putting.

I walk away shaking my head. And to think I wanted to put some money on this.

17

Be the Ball

I'm shooting about a 120 these days. But how do I *feel* about that?

Maybe I need to, you know, *see* someone about my golf game. A golf instructor, to be sure, but also maybe a . . . therapist. A shrink. A golf psychiatrist.

And, yes, of course there *are* golf psychiatrists. Have to be. People are *nuts* about golf. Noted golf psychiatrist Phil Lee was in my hometown hawking his book, *Shrink Your Handicap*, so I stopped by to see him, hoping for a free session, hoping he could take some strokes off my game.

Psychiatrists are MDs, of course. This means that Dr. Lee went to med school for years and years, and probably had to dissect a cadaver, suffer through his residency, and all the rest, only to wind up treating patients suffering not from cancer or broken arms or even psychoses, but rather from putting disorders.

I mean I could almost see it if Dr. Lee was trying to

cure people of their golf addictions (golf as avoidance mechanism, etc.), but he's trying to help them improve their scores. This is because he's One Of Them—a golf fiend.

"What about people who are addicted to golf," I ask, "people who play five times a week and in the snow and who neglect their jobs and their wives and kids to play golf?"

"And the problem with that is . . . ?" he smiles. He doesn't consider that to be a disorder, and if it is, "better to be addicted to golf than crack," he maintains. I don't know enough about crack to argue the point, but I doubt that it could be any more expensive or addictive or all-consuming than golf. Yet we have youth golf clinics to hook kids.

Dr. Lee looks to me like a golf psychiatrist should, be-spectacled, with a mustache, and wearing a golf shirt. And he says things like: "You know how Freud said it was all about sex? Now it's all about golf." Frightening. He says it's a mental game of hope versus fear, a game where one part of our brain is saying "play it safe," another part is saying "go for it!," and a third part is trying to balance the other two. (In addition some of us have a fourth brain part saying: "Run over your damned clubs with the car.")

I don't lie down right here in the Bookends bookstore or anything, but start telling the psychiatrist that I *feel* that my golf game sucks. When I tell him I shoot 120, he gets this alarmed look, like he might try to have me hospital-ized—or outfit my golf cart with a couch.

He says I probably have mental problems, and he cer-tainly wouldn't have a problem getting a concurring second opinion on that. He refers to my problem as: "a high mental handicap," although it was nothing that kept me out of the army or qualified me for an extra hour on my SATs.

The doctor says one can have "mental pars, mental birdies, or mental bogeys." He says throwing your clubs in the lake, for example, would be a "mental double bogey." However, if you hook it into the trees but chip out and recover—focused and calm—you can score a "mental eagle."

"Your mental handicap," Dr. Lee explains, "is the measure of the extent to which anxiety chemicals bring down your game. A million years ago, cavemen would go outside and see a saber-toothed tiger and become anxious and have chemical reactions that would make them better able to club the tiger or run away." He looks at me to see if I'm getting the picture. I give him a blank look that lets him know I'm not.

"Today," he continues, "when you see a water hazard on the golf course, you become anxious and your body releases small amounts of those same fight-or-flight chemicals that are poison to your golf game. Your muscles tighten, you breathe faster, your heart pounds harder, and your mind produces anxiety, anger, and fear."

Geez, what wimps we've become! How dull our existence, when we take small, decorative ponds on golf courses for saber-toothed tigers. I'm a little embarrassed for my species, frankly.

"You need to set up defenses to reduce those feelings of threat," he says. "We need to down-regulate our receptors and decrease our production of the chemicals that cause panic and anxiety." Would cocktails help?

He has another theory that our real golf game is never

as good as our "range game"—which is the way we play on the driving range or alone when no one's watching. This one I'm not so sure about, Doc. My range game sucks, too. And I'm pretty awful when no one's around. I admit it. I'm not one of those people who claim his parakeet can recite the Gettysburg Address except when people are around.

I tell Dr. Lee that I have a lot of trouble on the first tee, and I think it's because there are always people there watching.

Ah, yes, First Tee Anxiety Syndrome. "The first tee is the lair of the saber-toothed tiger," he says. This is a combination of Stranger Anxiety (fear of strangers), Subliminal Expectations (our friends won't accept us if we're bad), Generalization (we've been bad here before, we will be again), Superstition (start poorly and it will ruin the entire round), and Competitive Comfort Level (you're being judged by one shot because you haven't had the chance to make offsetting good shots).

Not to mention Generalized Tee Anxiety, in which "the golfer, flooded by chemicals from a million years ago, is diverted from his normal swing into a swing that is more primitive, more muscled, and more suited to clubbing an animal than to hitting a ball." We try to kill it. He recommends we loosen our grip and calm down.

When those fear chemicals are released, all of our senses become more acute and we are easily distracted. For this Dr. Lee advises we all get cassette recorders with headsets, record ourselves clapping, and add in some "Way to go!"s. Then, we listen to it when we're playing golf, listen to it over and over until it is no longer a distraction.

This is behavioral therapy teaching us not to be distracted. What about giving golfers a kernel of corn for a good shot and an electric shock for a bad one?

This cassette recorder therapy might replace, say, yelling at another foursome making a lot of noise while you're putting. "Hey a—holes! Shut up!" Or words to that effect. Then blaming them when you miss the putt.

Blame is bad, Dr. Lee says. Whenever we blame we are angry and that means more of those chemicals. Blame is bad and blame is complicated. In figuring out why we hook and slice and miss easy putts, he goes all the way back to unresolved conflicts in our childhood, when we spilled juice on the rug and Mommy scolded and blamed us. Yikes!

"Anything you are not supposed to do"—like hitting the ball into the woods!—"will lead to a scolding from Mommy," he says. "When we miss a shot in the presence of others, we attribute to them the disapproval we reflexively expect from others and we make mistakes. Or we scold ourselves. We get mad because we know we can do better. We 3-putt a hole and we blow up." Three-putting is a "balloon flaw" that can cause the whole rest of our round to go up in smoke.

It gets complicated and it gets deep. According to Dr. Lee, we apparently have to stop blaming our parents when we hit the ball into the sand. And I didn't even know I was.

When I hit a ball into the sand I usually say: "Bill, you stupid bastard. You hit the ball into the sand again." I never say: "Thanks a lot, *Mom!*" Who does that? Although, come to think of it, *Mom,* if you hadn't taught me to be so damned cautious all the time I might be all the way on the green instead of in the trap. Conversely, I might have been hit by a truck when I was four.

Dr. Lee says the sand trap can often be your parents' surrogate. You spill juice on the carpet, you hit the ball wrong, and you're punished and you're angry because it was an accident. Wow.

"All obstacles on the course continue to represent the parent and the anger is unresolved," the psychiatrist says. "To avoid having this continue to retard golf improvement, one must resolve anger at the parent. Stop blaming your parents and their surrogates: wind, water, and people who make noise when we putt. When we stop blaming our parents our golf game improves."

This would be your insight-oriented defense. I tried to put it into practice my next time out on the golf course. On my backswing I said out loud (because there are never any other golfers in the remote vicinities I play in): "Mom and Dad, if I hit this into one of the three sand traps surrounding the hole, I want you to know it's not your fault." But the damned ball went into the sand anyway. (For this I blame the course designer, who could more easily have placed one sand trap there, not three, and made thousands of golfers feel better.)

So what Dr. Lee says about your game improving when you stop blaming your parents may not hold true in all cases. As I attempted to hit out of the sand that third time, I thought I heard my long-departed father's voice from above: "Thanks, son, but I already realized it's not *my* fault. I told you *not* to play golf, you stupid little bastard."

Dr. Lee says an errant shot is not "wrong" and that we need to take "good" and "bad" out of our thinking. "To change the value setting on the 'bad' shot," he says, "we must reframe it as the 'unexpected' shot." Except, Doctor, that in my case the "bad" shot is not at all unexpected.

Dr. Lee wants us to regard the bad shot, rather the unexpected shot, as "a surprise." Not another piece-of-crap shot, but a lovely *surprise!* "Depending on your handicap," he writes in his book, "you can reasonably expect to be surprised on a golf course some predictable number of times per round."

But again, Doctor, for me quite the opposite holds true. It is the good shot that is the unexpected surprise—and a couple of times my unexpectedly good shots have nearly killed those playing ahead of me who never in their wildest dreams, or mine, thought I could hit a ball more than 150 yards.

To "reset my chemicals" on the "pre-shot" and get into "the zone," Dr. Lee tells me to practice by: lying down on my bed; focusing on breathing; relaxing, tightening, and relaxing my hands, shoulders, face, abs, buttocks, and legs; then forming my fingers in my customary grip on my golf club. This sounds very familiar, except one hand was always on a *Playboy* magazine. He suggests doing this for seven days in a row and using a real club. "Men Who Sleep With Their Golf Clubs"—next on Jerry Springer!

I would blame myself for not understanding all these things, but Dr. Lee told me not to blame myself. And he doesn't want me blaming myself for blaming myself either.

Getting back to that cassette recorder behavioral therapy, the doctor further suggests we might next want to record the "flash thoughts" that go through our minds as we address the ball, such as: "Stay clear of that water hazard"; "Don't think about all those idiots watching me"; "Why didn't I play with a bag over my head?"; and the like. Plus, he suggests we record the thoughts that we think are going through the minds of those who are watching us, for example: "He'll probably blow this shot, too"; "Why am I playing golf with this complete ass?"; "Bill probably has a short penis"—that type of thing.

Then, we play those messages over and over and over for what Dr. Lee refers to as "the magic hour," which is the time psychologists say we need to spend with our demons (be they snakes, spiders, or critics of our golf games) until we "turn off the anxiety/panic faucet" and no longer fear them.

Dr. Lee also offers a "cognitive" approach to dealing with those "Flash Golf Thoughts," which is to identify them and correct the ones that are unreasonable. That is, if your anxiety level about hitting the ball into the water is 80 percent, but the probability is really only 20 percent, you are overanxious and producing chemicals that will hurt your chances of actually avoiding the water.

He calls these "land mine thoughts," and through this cognitive approach tries to reduce them to simple mathematical probability problems.

In my case the probability is—quite probably—80 percent that I *will* hit the ball into the water. Indeed, like

171

Babe Ruth once did before hitting a home run, I've pointed to the water and accurately predicted exactly where my tee shot would land.

So, my ball still goes into the water, but using Dr. Lee's cognitive approach I am no longer anxious about it.

Thank you, Dr. Lee.

18

Tips for Beginners

Herewith a collection of some tips I'm picking up:

Always keep your own score. Remember, your best wood is your pencil.

If you slice right 45 degrees all the time, cancel that lesson with the club pro, and face left 45 degrees.

Remove those little knit booties from woods before using.

Don't bend over to tee up your ball with bag full of clubs over your shoulder or they'll spill out and make you look like Jerry Lewis.

It takes alotta balls to play like we do. Drop by the driving range and get a basketful from the machine before heading out to play 18 holes. That's about fifty balls, but you can always go back for more.

Don't be afraid to hit out of the club swimming pool.

Kids will scurry pronto when they see you wading in with a golf club, don't you worry.

Always drive the cart, so you can get to the scene first to "find" your ball in a favorable position.

Don't shout "You da man!" after someone hits, or sooner or later someone will kick your butt—and rightfully so.

Say "Shhhh" loudly while others putt—or alternatively, rattle change in your pocket, drop the flagstick, or break wind.

Have a designated driver. No, someone good to hit your drives for you.

Try to throw your ball underhand—more discreet.

Likewise, kick your ball as part of a natural, strolling motion.

Toss ball out of sand trap with a handful of sand for authenticity.

Carry orange traffic cones in your bag to stop traffic while you hit back across major thoroughfares.

When you mark your ball on the green put it back a lot closer to hole.

Never get your hopes up, no matter how great that last shot was.

Carry one cheap, old garage sale club to throw or break over your knee during temper tantrums.

Do not buy a $2,000 set of clubs. Shooting a 125 with those only makes matters worse—and besides: Do you really want high-tech clubs to make your balls go that much farther into the woods?

Don't be embarrassed about your 40–45 handicap.

The worse you are in golf the better your chance of winning—or something like that.

Use tees on every shot. Not putts, you'll never get away with it.

Every so often, skip a hole—still the fastest way we know to take 8 to 10 strokes off your game.

The number on the club does not necessarily mean that's the club you use all the time on that numbered hole.

Carry a paper bag in your golf bag big enough to fit over your head.

Lay flag on green behind hole to halt runaway putts.

Play with golfers of your own caliber, but wear a helmet.

Ask for a cart equipped with all-terrain vehicle tires. You'll be going where no golfer has gone before.

Similarly, pack a handheld global positioning system.

Take along a little something to eat, e.g., beef jerky, McDonald's fries, or other nonperishable foods.

Carry camping equipment—some holes give ground grudgingly and you might have to continue that assault on 14 in the morning.

And remember: Play your first 18 on the summer solstice, otherwise you'll run out of time.

19

Like Father, Like Son

Golf, they say, is a tie that binds: golfers and friends, golfers and wives, golfers and clients, golfers and absolute strangers.

Golfers and psychiatrists, golfers and bartenders, golfers and lending institutions, golfers and divorce lawyers.

Golfers and Sons. Now that would be a nice, heart-warming book in itself, wouldn't it? But that would not be this book. This book contains just this one, grisly chapter on this golfer and his son.

My father didn't teach me to play golf. He referred to golf as "pasture pool," a foolish waste of time to his way of thinking, and one for which God could not possibly have put us here on earth. A plausible argument, certainly, except Dad apparently *did* believe God intended us to instead be mowing the lawn properly and washing the car. It's possible. You know what they say about cleanliness.

He didn't approve of golf and he certainly didn't approve of the country club where the game was played. He didn't approve of drinking alcoholic beverages either, and those were the two predominant club activities offered to club members. Oh, they did play cards there, too, which Father referred to as "mental masturbation."

Now, this should not be just about fathers and sons playing golf together. I have a wonderful daughter, Libby, but she smartly limits her athletic activities with me. She was captain of her high school tennis team and she still plays, but not with me—probably for some of the same reasons I refuse to play with the cats: They can't return my shots and can't even hold their rackets correctly. She and I can't jog together because I don't. Or ski, because I don't ski, I tumble. Snow tumbling. Watch for it on ESPN2. And with regard to fishing together, Libby caught a bluefish while angling with her brother last summer and couldn't stop shrieking: "Ewwwwww!"

My son, Willie, was a high school football and basketball star, but minor sports have always posed problems—for both of us, especially when we're together. Fishing comes to mind. We rose at dawn to fish the hot spots in Canada and never caught a thing. We went fly-casting in Montana for eight hours with a guide and caught one trout—at a cost of about $275 a pound. We used to go out before dawn to surf-cast in Nantucket and not catch 'em. We'd keep coming home fishless, explaining: "Catch and release."

A defining moment was seeing my son, who was probably about fourteen, one chill summer's morn, standing fifty feet away in the fog, knee-deep in the Atlantic, and casting, casting, casting . . . As he reeled in perhaps his hundredth fruitless try, he called out to me over the sound of the surf:

"Hey, Dad!"

"Yes, son."

"This reeeally sucks!"

"Yes, son. Yes it does." Suck.

Our golfing partnership began in a small, miniature way on vacations at Lake George, Nantucket, the Outer Banks, and Myrtle Beach, which is probably the miniature golf capital of the world. You want your children to see that. The game was a lot of laughs, until he became a full-blown teenager, competitive, and a little surly when he missed "crucial" shots.

The first non–miniature golf we played together was when he was about eight years old, on a par-3 course adjacent to a bed-and-breakfast in New Hampshire (or possibly that other one, Vermont). I don't remember a whole lot about that golf game, but I do have disturbing flashbacks to hitting a mean slice into the side of a lovely Victorian farmhouse: THWACK! And I remember creeping up to the house and tiptoeing around on the porch looking for the ball, because we only had one ball each. I retrieved it from under a wicker chair. Luckily nobody was home. Civil Defense personnel had probably evacuated the neighborhood after observing us on the previous hole.

Willie was naturally a little embarrassed, but also highly amused. I remember laughing a lot during the ordeal, and discovering that here I not only had this wonderful son, but at the same time was growing a good friend, a kindred spirit with a great, albeit twisted, sense of humor.

He and I played a few times in Siasconset on Nantucket, which may sound a bit stuffy but was anything but. It was a public course in the pure sense, played by golfers in inappropriately awful attire and with golf games to match. This was back when Nantucket was still painfully unpretentious, when the smaller your whaler's cottage, the older and more rusted-out your Jeep, the more prestigious. Now the public course is adjacent to a new private golf club that costs more than $200,000 to join and is played by golfers building gargantuan Marriott-sized homes or coming in for the round by private jet.

Back then, a round of golf at that public course cost—what?—twelve bucks, maybe, plus the cost of renting clubs. One did not own clubs at our level. We rented what always seemed to be the last set they had. The guy in the little shack there where you paid your money would kind of scrounge around in a little closet to come up with what was more or less a set of clubs that was also painfully unpretentious. Prewar. Possibly the Great War, conceivably Spanish-American. The putter was deeply scarred as if it might have been used to change truck tires. The driver was wooden, with screws sticking so far out of the bottom that if you swung properly they could actually dig into the turf and bring the club to a complete stop before it struck the ball. Almost like a restraint system. Best to bring some power tools to ready these rental units for play. But all in all, the equipment was a pretty good match for our level of play.

We spent a lot on balls, however, usually buying the

family thirty-six-pack for 9 holes. No sense in buying too few. Willie and I would walk outside and sit on the bench, waiting for the coast to clear. We refused to tee off if anyone was around to watch. It didn't hurt our game, it hurt our feelings. I recall both of us diving back to the bench once when a car drove into the parking lot.

There was a sign over the bench reading "No Nuisance Golfers," but luckily they didn't post photographs the way they do at the post office and no one knew we were offenders. Willie and I would always look at the sign, look at each other, and shrug. I mean we weren't intentionally nuisance golfers, certainly, and we weren't nuisance golfers 100 percent of the time.

Sometimes we'd sit on that bench for quite a while before garnering enough courage to step to the first tee to smack our wretched drives. We usually felt a lot better after watching a few others tee off ahead of us. This day a gentleman ahead of us shanked one, as they say, hitting it to his right at an angle of about 45 degrees. His shot made it all the way to the green, a magnificent shot, except it was not on the 1st green, but rather the 6th, I believe—and nearly a hole-in-one!

We laughed a little, couldn't help ourselves, and were immediately punished by the godless golf gods. The guy in the shack came out and said we had to double up and play with two other golfers, our worst nightmare. This would ruin our whole day—not to mention theirs. Yes, it takes pretty much the whole day for us to play 9 holes.

And a perfect little pair they were, too, a matched set: a handsome, well-scrubbed husband and wife in their early thirties, tanned and fit, wearing nifty sun visors bearing the name of their country club back home—"You'll-Never-Smell-It Hills," or something—dressed in coordinated tan and forest green outfits, wielding shiny new clubs (with little tan and green mittens on the clubheads) nestled in buttery leather bags, and sporting snazzy golf shoes made from some endangered species.

"But, but . . ." I sputtered, "we don't really know how to *play*. We'll just hold you up."

"No problem," said the perfectly polite man, possibly Chad. "We don't mind at all."

I hate that! Good golfers are always deigning to spout that kind of good-sport, patronizing poppycock. Or do golfers actually take fiendish enjoyment in watching others struggle more than they?

The best Willie and I could hope for was that they were all show—no go, or that at least the attractive young woman would be somewhat awful. Or not wearing underwear. Something! Unfortunately this was the type of woman who probably wore two sets, and moreover she went first and hit a long, looong, straight-straight, perfect-perfect drive, which her charming husband matched. "Well done," she remarked.

"Oh, shit," I said, sotto voce, to my son, who I could tell wanted very badly to leave. I suppose I should have said something genteel like "I'm sorry, my son has diarrhea," and begged off. "I think it was the lobster fra diavolo."

But in my state of shock I instead walked almost comatose to the tee, put down my ball, and looked calmly down the fairway, for a moment thinking that maybe, just maybe, if I pretended to be one of them, I'd hit the ball as they had.

In sports it's called "visualization" and it can work, sports psychologists agree. So I stepped up confidently, struck the ball, and you know what? In baseball it would have been a nice line shot single over the shortstop's head. Maybe things got mixed up in the Visualization Department in my brain; maybe my visualization papers were filed under the wrong sport or something. I mean, Jesus, the mind is a labyrinthine mumbo-jumbo of entangled wires and circuits. So, here, my line shot baseball hit was a line shot golf hook into the bushes. And you know what? Willie matched my drive, too, just as the husband matched the wife's, which I found to be very considerate on his part. His drive was a bit farther at least, farther into the bushes.

We began beating the bushes with our clubs, but it was Chad who spotted our balls. We emerged from the thicket bowed and bleeding and pleading with the lovely couple to play on without us. But they stayed with us for several holes, probably by the same principle that you don't just stay for five minutes when you do volunteer work at the old folks home. Finally they realized that we might not finish before dark and bid us adieu. The way they hit the ball they were out of sight, at warp speed, in seconds.

At the next tee, a charming older woman came over and raved about the "Sunday Morning" television program that I'm part of, then she teed off while we waited for them to get safely ahead. It was a short, par-3 hole so we waited until she and her partner were all the way on the green, putting, before we hit our drives.

Somehow—somehow—my ball took off for distance, and somehow—somehow—directly at the green. Perhaps the Visualization Department found my order.

"Oh no!" I gasped. "What's that word . . . ?"

"Fore!" Willie yelled, as my ball zipped not three feet past her head. She turned around, this fan of mine, and gestured, possibly with her middle finger. She was pretty far away. But I could see her shaking her head as she walked off the green.

How the hell was I supposed to know? How was I to know that I—I!—would hit a great drive? Sometimes good shots happen to bad golfers.

Anyway I was in the zone, baby. I accidentally parred the next hole, a straight fairway with no hazards. I found the scorecard and penciled that one in. Willie congratulated me, somewhat insincerely. I felt guilty, like I was cruelly breaking a pact with my own son, a pact that we'd both be bad for so long as we both shall live. If anyone had the luck, I wanted it to be him. Well, not really . . .

I didn't have to ponder that ethical dilemma for long. I went into a bit of a slump for the next, say, hour and a half. That's the thing about golf. You hit a decent shot, or maybe even three in a row for a par, and you think that maybe you've finally found the groove, once and for all.

But of course you haven't. It's just luck. It's like shooting craps in Vegas and winning a few rolls before going on a losing streak from 11:00 P.M. to 4:00 A.M. You're making out like a bandit with the complimentary cocktails and the $5.99 all-you-can-eat buffet, but suddenly you're out five grand.

Willie was particularly frustrated. He's a natural athlete accustomed to excelling at "real" sports. He had played twice before on this vacation, had improved the second time, and assumed he'd play even better this time. But, no. That's not the way o' the links.

His problem may have had something to do with the fact that he is six foot four, and his rental clubs might have previously belonged to former Secretary of Labor Robert Reich—the one who you always thought hadn't shown up for his press conference but was really there behind the podium.

At last, we reached the final tee, he and I. With dusk falling, I hit a chopper down the third base line and decided to take another try. A mulligan, I believe. And another. A mcmulligan? An O'Shaughnessy? I'm not sure what they call that third try. And another. Erin go bragh! This was turning into a St. Patrick's Day parade of drives.

Then my son stepped up and hit a beauty—an awesomely powerful drive, perhaps 250 or even 300 yards, plus a great roll after it hit the highway. Then he hit another, and another, and another, until a groundskeeper came over the top of the hill on an all-terrain vehicle. He was probably a member of a search party dispatched to see if those two guys who rented the clubs hours and hours before were somehow still out there at sundown hacking away.

He was shouting something. Was there an emergency of some kind? No . . .

"Move it!" he was yelling. "This isn't a driving range!"

We moved along, Willie and I, the two of us taking turns advancing the one ball we had left. The final 9th hole yielded ground grudgingly, like the Japanese soldiers dug into those hilltop machine gun nests in *The Thin Red Line*.

It grew late. It was starting to look like we might have to pitch camp and attack the green at dawn.

"Dad," Willie said in the gathering darkness.

"Yes, son."

"I hate golf."

"So do I, son. I think we all do."

"It reeeally sucks."

"Yes, son. It really does." Suck.

20

Big Bertha and Me

I should probably be buying my own clubs by now, although rental clubs do have their advantages. They're a great excuse for playing badly and you can abuse them like you do rental cars.

They say the right clubs can be good for another 10 strokes off your game. (That's 78!) And maybe I really would play a lot better with clubs custom-fit to my physique (maybe with shafts that curve out a little at the abdominal area) and to my personal inability level. I've seen advertisements touting certain clubs as "forgiving." I like that. You used to have to go to church for that stuff.

The term golf *clubs* bothers me. Shouldn't they be called golf "instruments," or "implements," or golf "tackle," or golfing "rods," or "utensils," or even "sticks" the way they're called in hockey and lacrosse—something a little more delicate than clubs?

Tiger doesn't *club* his ball, he strokes it, fades it, draws it, feathers it, lofts it, spins it, taps it in. Although, in my case, *clubs* may be the more accurate term. Considering the level of refinement I bring to the game, I should probably purchase a single fat, gnarly club like those the cavemen ran around with beating on woolly mammoths.

But, what to buy? There's a single adjustable club that performs the functions of fourteen, from driving to putting. There are clubs that guarantee backspin, clubs that cost $600 apiece, and clubs made from armor-piercing steel that you can fire bullets at without hurting them. But why? I think it's to show how strong they are, but who among us has not wanted at some point to gun down our golf clubs?

Manufacturers spend tens of millions of dollars on golf club research every year to create clubs so advanced that they practically play the game for you. Someday you won't even have to show up. As a matter of fact, the testing is done in laboratories using robots to hit the balls, and I would like to know if we can purchase the robots as well as the clubs.

I want that kind of club, the kind that takes me out of the equation: big, fat-headed drivers that give you a slingshot effect. Woods and irons that promise not to slice or hook, and ones that loft the ball even when you top it. They're out there. Of course those are the ones that cost the most. And there's probably nothing worse than a guy like me with a $1,500 set of clubs chalking up a 125.

They sell golf clubs everywhere these days. You can get 'em at BJ's Price Club or Costco, right next to the forty-five-pound tins of pepper and the fifty-five-gallon drums of ketchup. Big clubs. Cheap. Just don't ask for advice from the guy stocking the shelves with the forty-eight-packs of horseradish. And you may have to buy drivers in a twelve-pack.

You can buy clubs on the Internet, of course, and you can find them in the classifieds, and at country club pro shops (with the customary 300 percent markup), and at one of those big Golf Galaxy Super Mega Outlet Warehouse stores that are springing up everywhere you look.

I wandered through one of those Golf World–type stores, trying in vain to fend off helpful (aka on commission) salesclerks. One finally snagged me and opened up on me with a barrage of terms like "kick point" and "swing weight" and "stem torsion" and "dual weight ports." It was that same feeling you get when you're buying a new computer from a nineteen-year-old techno-geek. I felt myself reaching my own personal kick point and fled before I lashed out at him.

It's terribly confusing. Woods are not wood anymore, irons not iron. Everything is titanium these days. The big golf club manufacturing area in southern California is called the Titanium Coast. Even the golf *gloves* at BJ's claim to be titanium. Considering my drives go about a hundred yards, I'm more in the market for plutonium— turbo plutonium.

It's like the 10 billion bottles of water allegedly coming out of the little Evian spring in France. Can there possibly be this much titanium in the world? Aren't our precious titanium reserves being dangerously depleted? Aren't the United Titanium Mine Workers overworked and underpaid—if, as we suspect, it is in fact mined? And aren't they suffering from Gray Lung Disease? What if titanium is leeching through the skin of golfers and causing inoperable palm disease? And what if our kids suck on our clubs and score poorly on their SATs? So many questions. How little we know of this ubiquitous and enigmatic element!

There are scary new rogue forms of titanium, such as Black Titanium, "the next generation of titanium," which actually guarantees no hooks or slices. But at what price? Science can grow four-hundred-pound tomatoes that glow and throb on the vine, too, but would you eat a BLT that moves?

There are ominous signs that our reserves—hell, most of them are in Russia!—may already be running out. Cubic Balance is watering down its titanium clubs with zirconium and calling it "Tizirc." Other club-makers are blending it with tungsten or forgoing titanium altogether and using beryllium copper.

The newest clubs are being made of steel, which used to be considered horribly outdated, but now is not. It has been rediscovered so that everyone will replace their titanium clubs. Callaway has "Steelhead Plus," Taylor Made touts its "Supersteel," and Kasco "guarantees" you'll never, ever slice a ball again thanks to "super hytech" steel.

All of this space-age technology focused on my pitiful little golf game. Golf scientists from our best research universities—who really should be doing something more important, shouldn't they?—recently announced an important breakthrough in the discovery of an alloy of titanium, zirconium, nickel, copper, and beryllium in which the particles aren't arrayed in crystalline patterns that come together in pattern boundaries to form weak spots in typical metals. So, Mr. Lab Coat, why does my ball still sail into the damned bunkers?

And all these numbers! The old 1–9 irons seem to be on the way out, being replaced by a whole new numbering system: loft degrees. Celsius? Fahrenheit? Who knows? You want the 8.5 degree wood? These trajectory comparison charts and center of gravity graphs should be of some help. How about a 21 degree rescue club? Does the 55 or the 56 degree wedge sound better to you? Wedges used to be sand or pitch but now come in at least 12 degree differentials, some touting "15 percent greater inertia." You want that inertia out there working for you every day, brother. The drivers come in 6, 7, 8, 9, 10, 11, or 12 degree loft. What's your pleasure? Hmmm?

And the putters! Taylor Made alone has eleven models of the Nubbins putter featuring the "proprietary insert compound" that golfer Gary McCord says "reminds me of a gummy bear"—and we all know they're good. Ping offers about forty styles of putters, such as the Isoforce 2 2000 with the pixilated copper insert, a significant improvement on the nickel-titanium insert. There is the Hog putter, featuring a fat grip, fat shaft, and fat head that was recently okayed by St. Andrews (the golfing club, not the saint himself). Callaway offers sixteen kinds with features such as the double radius shaft bend, low flex reverse taper shaft, and the offset hosel—just like President Clinton! If Monica is to be believed.

At the golf merchandise show, I saw some really odd ones, like blown glass putters, a two-shafted putter, and the Sight Wing putter with a shiny parabolic-shaped reflector on the head like the Lunar Explorer vehicle so you can see the hole when looking at the ball—and probably bring in 500 TV channels at the same time. There's the Fazer Putter with two red lights on top that come on when you're perfectly lined up. But nothing quite so strange as Pure Bull Peter Putters. That's right, the shafts are "made from the reproductive organ of American bulls." Buy American. "Only quality, handpicked bull organs are used." Employees must wash hands. "Finds the hole every time." And what happens then?

For our fifth golf class in the gym, Liz had invited a salesman from a golf store to talk to us about purchasing clubs and his first words were prescient: "Buying clubs is very confusing." Not like renting, where they might ask you "lefty or righty?"—or they might not. "We have one hundred different sets in our store," he says. "Prices range from $200 a set to $2,000. You can spend $1,300 just for a set of irons, $360 or more for a single driver."

Questions arise: "What's in a set?" asks a student. He said a set normally includes the P, not the S, three woods, eight irons, and a putter. He said the driver is a wood. He said this because he knew we were idiots.

"Titanium or steel?" The salesman recommends stainless steel clubs for beginners, predicting we'd be hitting a lot of rocks and dirt and asphalt—"and my husband," added the student who said her husband tried to teach her something on every swing.

"What's with all the different shafts?" He explains that

the new "bubble shafts" offer more speed and less deflection—deflection apparently being a bad thing.

With irons, he says we definitely want to purchase hollow backs: "They have much larger sweet spots, which used to be the size of the tip of your pinkie, but are now the size of two golf balls. Clubs today are much more forgiving. Bigger clubs are more forgiving. They require less skill." Forgiveness is divine, bigger is better, less skill is just the ticket.

He says the Ping ISI, for example, is a huge driver, 323 cubic centimeters: "It has that trampoline effect and was almost outlawed by the USGA." (Another driver, the new Callaway ERC, has been banned by the USGA for its spring effect.) I definitely want stuff that is almost or absolutely illegal. But if the Ping is $380, and if you do indeed . . . suck . . . as we do . . . it just means you're going to be hitting the ball that much farther into surrounding communities.

My head is spinning. His store has two hundred different putters ($15 to $300) to consider, not to mention shoes ($40 to $250) and bags ($60 to $300) and gloves and balls and umbrellas and scoops to get balls out of the water and all the other necessities. I think I prefer basketball, where you just buy a ball.

Liz reminds us that no matter how much we spend, there are no guarantees, and that we can't return the clubs simply because $800 or $2,000 later we continue to . . . suck.

"You can have $2,000 clubs and a $2 game," the salesman says. "You can't buy a game."

"Well *that's* discouraging!" blurts one student, who left and never came back.

21

It Takes Alotta Balls

Are your balls reactive?" asks the hawker, as we pass by his booth at the PGA show.

Excuse me? Is this the Ramrod Bar in New York or the PGA Golf Merchandise Show?

"Your golf balls," he adds, by way of clarification.

"No, I don't think so," I reply, after some reflection. "Passive, I would say. Sometimes when I swing at them they go nowhere at all."

"Well," he says, "our Ram Tour Reactive ball has the 'magic metal' neodymium core, the most explosive core in golf for maximum distance or your money back."

Neodymium? Sounds like the ring I bought Jody in the precious stones department at Kmart.

"Or," he says, "you could go with the Balata LB with the blend of titanium and lithium balata and the patented 442 dimple pattern. Or the XV2, a blend of titanium, magnesium, and neodymium with the patented neodymium and polybutadiene core for the softest feel and maximum spin?"

Huh? Lithium balata? Sounds like a really slow Latin dance. Or the stuff they give hyperactive fourth-grade boys to turn them into desks.

Polybutadiene I think I've heard of. Might be that orange dust on Cheez-Kurls.

He also has the XOC, which comes in orange, yellow, or raspberry, but I tell him I think there's probably enough snickering when I play already, thanks.

The Volvik booth offers the four-piece metal model 432 octahedron with the bismuth mixed dual power core and the zirconium cover. Bismuth? That's a "miracle substance" (as well as the fine capital of the Minnesota–North Dakota area).

Or perhaps I'd prefer the Air Channel ball with "no-slice technology"—Ha!—and "explosive distance." Ha-ha! You see, "the Air Channel connecting dimples reduce excessive air drag for more distance and reduce side spin for reduced slice and hook factors." The Wright brothers had less research data for their flight than these balls do.

Titleist has an enormous golf ball exhibit at the show, festooned with huge billboards of pros like David Duval hitting Titleist balls. The exhibit features about twenty computer terminals where you can enter your golf game attributes and problem areas (m-y-g-a-m-e-s-u-c-k-s), and the computer tells you what kind of (Titleist) golf balls to buy. In my case the computer urged me to buy floating golf balls, a lot of golf balls, and a tetherball so I could just move on to another sport altogether.

The next booth has *irradiated* balls! They're described

as "the world's longest legal balls." I check the package to see if there's a warning that their irradiated balls might affect mine—lowering sperm count, causing erectile dysfunction, that type of thing. Not that it would matter. Golfers would gladly risk a short putz for longer drives. As you'll recall from history class, on June 30, 1999, in Tenerife on the Canary Islands, British golfer Karl Woodward drove the irradiated TNT ball (with the high-energy XD core and the Surlyn cover and exclusive cross-linked Dura-Shield coating) a historic and almost unbelievable four hundred eight yards and ten inches! Apparently, in one shot. Sort of like when they tested the irradiated hydrogen bomb on a remote island in the South Pacific. Four hundred and eight! But isn't June hurricane season in the Canaries? Karl probably carried a good three hundred yards down the fairway himself.

On display here, too, are special balls just for putting, like the Bald Eagle, with several "undimpled striking points," because "striking a dimple ridge can throw off a putt 5 degrees or more." But how you go about exchanging that great putting ball for the "world's longest legal ball" that got you to the green, without your partners noticing, isn't outlined in the colorful brochure. You'll have to figure that one out yourself. Also, I'm not so sure that I don't want my putts thrown off 5 degrees.

Sadly, there are no magnetized balls that are just drawn to the tin cup, but there is the EZ-Reader ball with a built-in bubble level window to show you the slope of the green. And there are "guidance system" balls with arrows painted on them to show you that your ball is rolling true.

Could any of these things possibly be legal? And, if

they're so hot, why doesn't Tiger Woods use any of this crap?

There are training balls with badminton feathers so you can swing away in the backyard without those reckless endangerment charges being filed by the neighbors . . . trick exploding balls . . . balls with your former spouse's picture on them . . . Eco-Golf balls, which decompose in fresh- or saltwater within ninety-six hours with no toxic or hazardous residues left behind (but how does that help *me?*) . . . glow-in-the-dark golf balls . . . floating—yes!— golf balls . . . and the Golden Girl ball for "older women with slower swings," which I would definitely buy if the words "Golden Girl" weren't printed on them . . . and the Won-Putt ball, brazenly claiming it "saves 3–10 strokes per round"!

Good Balls: -3–10 strokes per round. That's 81–88 strokes off my game so far. I'm closing in on par!

22

Cutting Your Losses

Now, you don't have to spend a fortune buying all these clubs and balls *new*. In fact, it's suggested that novices might want to consider used equipment, because at first we do tend to abuse our clubs and lose our balls. We don't call them *used*, of course, any more than we call used cars used. We call them "pre-driven" or one of the "encore series."

As mentioned, we like to shop at Grandpa Brennan's Previously Owned Golf Ball Emporium, owned and operated by Jerry, his wife, Peggy, their children and grandchildren. He has a prime location, albeit a dangerous one, adjacent to Goat Hill. They live there, too, just a two-hundred-yard slice from the second tee, not more than ten or fifteen yards from the fairway just across a little two-lane road. Love Canal might be safer.

Merchandise is displayed on a table in the yard, separated into the three-for-a-dollars (to include balata and titanium balls) kept in a wooden case or twelve-pack egg cartons, and the five-for-a-dollars in a dish strainer. "It's a quality difference," Jerry explains, with some of the five-for-a-dollars showing a slight blemish here and there. At either price, it's a deep discount, representing substantial savings over new balls that sell for from one dollar to more than four dollars apiece these days.

Jerry's balls bear the names of individuals, banks, beers, investment houses, country clubs, and fast-food restaurants, as well as encouragements to "Go For It!" and to "Just Say No." In addition to the classic white, the balls come in every color not in the rainbow, such as fluorescent yellow, shocking pink, and roadwork-ahead orange.

As we're shopping, there is a sharp, loud CRACK! as an errant tee shot hits the road ten feet away and bounces onto the Brennans' roof. "Did they get ya?" Jerry laughs as he comes out of the house. I'm having a damned flashback to 'Nam—"Incoming!"—but Jerry's jocular tone snaps me out of it. He shows me the side of his house, the one facing teeward, which is riddled with holes, some the size of golf balls, others larger.

"Bullet holes," he remarks with a chuckle. "There's some real beauties."

His wife, Peggy, thinks it's funny, too. "We're thinking of having the grandkids wear helmets when they come over," she says, and the two of them laugh together. Peggy has been hit, and her friend's car window smashed here.

The family collects balls from the yard and goes ball-hawking on the course. There are eight kids and eleven grandchildren, who all join in, equipped with long poles meant to fetch balls from water hazards, but which work equally well in the brier patches. Jerry won't reveal his best spots, any more than clammers around here will reveal theirs. It's fertile ground. The public course attracts some really bad players, like myself, and there are no caddies to watch the flight of the ball.

Jerry is a retired teacher who started the business to make some money in the summer. He sells about 4,500 balls a year now. "Many are repeaters," Jerry says. "Sometimes we sell the same ball over and over and over."

Jerry sells us some balls as we head for the course. "I think I'll be seeing these balls again," he quips. I write "Hi Jerry" on one with a marker.

There are used club dealers, too. I'm driving along a two-lane road on the North Fork of Long Island when I spot a small display of golf bags, clubs, and balls sitting in a front yard. I hit the brakes and pull into the driveway of Reg Peterson, whose porch and yard comprise a show-room of golf equipment.

He ball-hawks, too, in the woods surrounding Island's End Golf Club down the road, and has thousands of clean, like-new golf balls—sorted by brand and type—to show for it. He found four thousand last year. He offers Pinnacles at $6 a dozen, Titleists for $7, and Taylor Mades for $8. He has the new Callaways for 60 cents a piece—the ones that sell new for $4.40 each!

"Some of these have only been hit once," he claims. Reg knows this because he's seen them leave the course off the first tee. "I was out hawking one day and watched a guy hit a ball seven times in a sand trap before he finally picked up his ball and threw it at *me*. He said I was making him nervous watching him"—and after all, Reg is a bit like the Grim Reaper of Golf. "He said I had no business on a golf course, and I told him he certainly didn't either."

Where did all the clubs come from? He finds some of those in the woods, too. "Most of those I find are snapped in two by angry golfers," he says, "but sometimes guys are so mad they just fling 'em into the woods." He wishes he could get at those water hazards, a favorite destination when disgruntled golfers hurl their clubs.

He gets some of his club inventory from garage sales or those special big trash days when homeowners can set anything they don't want on the curb for pickup. And some people really don't want their golf clubs anymore.

"People start to dislike the game and can't wait to get rid of them," he says. "You'd be surprised."

"Not really," I reply.

"These old clubs are better than all these newfangled ones," he says, taking a handsome wooden wood out of a bag there in the yard and caressing it. "They sound better and feel better when you hit the ball. These metal things sound like those awful aluminum bats they use in baseball. The major leagues don't use them for a reason. That ping and clink drives me nuts."

Whereas new woods and irons can easily cost $100, $200, $300 or more *apiece,* Reg is selling woods for $16 and irons for $7. He's offering a complete set of clubs in an attractive (to some) baby blue bag for $100. He has a complete line of golfing equipment, including left-handed sets. He even has shoes, although this being the height of the season and everything right now he has just the two pair and both are women's eight and a halfs.

You ever hear of those super sports stores like the one in the Mall of America where you can try out your clubs in the store? Reg has had that for years, right there in his side yard. He even has a hole with a flag in it.

He's been in the business twenty-seven years, although he gave up actually playing golf five years ago when he made a hole-in-one.

"I quit right then and there," he says. "I never was much good at the game." And fortunately for him and the missus, most other golfers aren't either.

23

A Few Modest Proposals

There are a few things I'd change about golf. Playing the closest hole, rather than being locked into that whole numbered hole thing, would be first and foremost on my list of changes, but golf could also use some other improvements like a few more holes in each green for players like me. And par. Par's got to go. No other sport has par. It makes 99.9 percent of all golfers feel bad.

If it is to continue posing as a bona fide professional *sport*, golf needs a lot of work. It's time to bring this sport or hobby or skill or whatever it is into the twenty-first century, to ensure its TV viability, and maybe finally get it into the Olympics, where every other conceivable form of human *activity* is on display, to include synchronized swimming, where the "athletes" wear sequins and blue eye makeup, and that one where people run around in their leotards with streamers and rubber balls.

Right now watching golf on TV is tantamount to tending an aquarium. Herewith, a few modest proposals to get golf *moving*.

Golf is the only sport with carts, so perhaps the game should be *played* in them, with golfers hitting their balls from moving carts, polo-style. This, plus the added possibility of playing polo golf with lots of players and just one ball, possibly in teams, with a "goal" of a green and cup at either end. Most sports have goals at either end: football, basketball, hockey, soccer. And with teams you'd have uniforms. Get out of those earth-tone polo shirts, willya? Get some cool uniforms. Black and teal. You know.

If they insist upon sticking to regular individual golf, maybe on the 18th a goalie could run onto the green as the putt was rolling and try to make a diving save. Introduce a little *defense* to golf. Like every other sport. Imagine Tiger trying to hit a fairway shot with somebody *guarding* him. Goalies and defensemen, that's better.

Maybe throw a few windmills on the greens to make things more interesting. Or cross golf with a little croquet so that you could hit your opponent's golf ball, and "send" it into the bushes or the water hazard. Hazards could stand to be a little more interesting, too. Instead of sand, how about Jell-O chocolate pudding in those bunkers? And if traditionalists insist on sand, why not *quick*sand. That would speed things up.

Pick up the pace! Golf would be a better game for fans, certainly, and better for players, too, if we didn't have so much damned time to *think*. How about a time clock? Fastest to play 18 holes wins. Get a little running going out on the course. Almost every sport has running. (Except the two-man luge, which still has the lying.) If you had running you'd have sweating. Almost all sports have that. With running and sweating, you'd have substitutes and benches and coaches and *plays*. Golf plays: "Tiger drives it way over the head of the defender to Duval, who darts past another defenseman, drops the ball, and chips it onto the green, where Mickelson buries the putt!"

Fans go wild. Right now, golf fans never go wild. They're told to be quiet all the time and the announcers have to whisper. There should be booing at golf matches, and when a fella mis-hits and ruins his chances in a tournament, the gallery should let him have it: "Na-na-na-na, na-na-na-na, hey-hey, goo-ood bye!" When someone's putting, fans should be yelling and waving their arms. There should be cheerleaders and pep bands. And bonfires!

Not to mention brawls. A pro hits a 300-yard drive, the second guy hits one 350, the first guy throws down his club and goes after him. Sure. Let's see a little emotion out there! How about when a pro golfer tees off, his opponent gets to take a shot at the drive with a shotgun? Skeet-golf.

How about Extreme Golf, with Vince McMahon, head of the World Wrestling Federation, running the Masters in Augusta? He'd have stronger characters, in flashy outfits, with names like Hole-In-Juan, Course Buster, and Par Force!

Or Obstacle Golf, where players have to climb over fifteen-foot walls and swing on ropes across crocodile-infested water hazards to get to their next shots. That would liven things up. And for ratings: Survivor Golf, played on an uninhabited island off Borneo, a marathon golf match, 500 holes, over a month's time with no water and no food save for beetle larvae and roasted rats!

Yes! I'm going to talk to golf's governing body, the Royal and Ancient Golf Club of St. Andrews, Scotland, about just that.

24

The Bad Golfers Association National Tournament

Maybe I could win a tournament, a national tournament, a national tournament of the very worst golfers in America: the Bad Golfers Association Open in Kansas City.

Have you ever asked yourself, perhaps after a particularly heinous shot, "Just how bad *am* I?" I mean, you know you're bad, but you'll never really know how bad until you've put your skills to the test against the worst of the worst.

At the BGA Open bad golfers are given the opportunity to do just that—if you qualify. The BGA was founded a few years ago by two of the worst golfers I've ever seen, John McMeel, president of Universal Press Syndicate, and Pat Oliphant, the renowned political cartoonist, after they'd played another miserable round of golf together, one in which Pat had watched the head of his (rented) driver fly into a Florida swamp.

"We decided that we were so spectacularly bad," says McMeel, "we wanted to somehow honor that by organizing."

"And," Oliphant chimes in, "why should the game of golf be left in the hands of a bunch of grim-faced over-achievers? Have you ever seen anybody *smile* on the PGA circuit? They're the wrong role models"—apparently implying that he and McMeel are, somehow, the right ones.

"There are more of us than there are of them," McMeel concludes, noting that about 27 million people play golf and only an estimated 10 percent shoot 100 or better.

He said bad golf is part of our heritage, and you could almost hear the fife and drum as we recounted together such historic summits as that of Presidents Clinton, Ford, and Bush playing together in the Bob Hope Chrysler Classic, the one where Ford hit one spectator and Bush hit two, a ricochet shot off a tree that broke a woman's glasses and gave her ten stitches in her nose.

Thank God we live in America. They say that in the Netherlands golfers need to pass a test and hold a golf ability card. They must hit three drives straight more than 130 yards, hit five approach shots to within four and a half yards of the cup, and putt five balls from eleven yards out to within six feet of the hole! Thank God they didn't win the war!

I'd phoned McMeel to detail my qualifications and credentials for winning a slot in the BGA tournament. "You seem more than qualified," he said, just halfway through my presentation, which seemed flattering and insulting at the same time.

Upon arriving in Kansas City, Jody (who was thinking

of playing in the *W*BGA tournament) can't help but be impressed. These guys are serious about bad golf. They have all the trappings of the PGA, including a complete line of products—calendars, mugs, golf shirts, and such— all bearing the official BGA crest, which shows a bent putter and a wreath of poison ivy atop the motto "Bad But Proud." The night before the tourney there is a lavish soiree at the Ritz-Carlton. Everything about the BGA is first-class—except, of course, the golf.

The BGA Open brings together 132 bad golfers from throughout the country, who feel a need to test their own ineptitude against that of other low-notch incompetents. This is more than a contest, however, it is a chance for the golf-challenged to meet others with similar handicaps and to share their experiences, unashamedly, the way other kinds of freaks do on Jerry Springer. For some, it's a chance to merely play golf with other people, since no one wants to play with them at home.

"Their love of the game just exceeds their ability to play, that's all," notes McMeel, who probably should be fighting back tears.

A group of us sit in the shade and talk about our appalling golf games before the Open begins, a time when we probably should be practicing or slamming down Bloody Marys.

The first to speak says he wishes he could play with a bag over his head. "I stand up to the ball and have absolutely no idea what's going to happen when I hit it," says the strapping young man. "It might go 5 feet or 270 yards. I've hit surrounding houses so hard the balls come back on the fairway. I can't understand it. Why would anyone build a house just 220 yards from a golf course?"

"Well," I note, "that *is* an eighth of a mile." He puts his head down and nods.

"I've broken windows in houses," blurts out another golfer, and you can see the first guy already feels a little better. This is turning into something of a support group.

"I'm so bad I destroy the clubs," says another. "One time the head fell off my driver and another time I borrowed a 7-iron from a friend and slung it by accident into a pond and had to go in after it. It's embarrassing swimming around in front of other golfers."

Two lay claim to the title "worst golfer in Kansas City," something that will be decided this day on the field of play. One of these men says his biggest drawback is that his wife won't let him play on weekends. The other says he is the worst golfer in K.C. because he doesn't cheat. "Honesty," he proclaims, "is a major handicap in golf, obviously." Words to the wise.

Others in this group therapy session describe themselves as "the worst you've ever seen," "the worst golfer you've ever met," and so forth. It was an illustrious-free field. All are well known in their local communities as very bad golfers. A guy named Becker from Seattle has set a personal goal of proving here that he is the worst in the world and says: "I should have my own organization: the Really Bad Golfers Association." Some say they've never kept score, but Becker says he shoots in the "85 to 150" range, which means if he has a bad (i.e., a good, low-scoring) day he won't stand a chance.

But none said they would stoop to cheating to be the worst. "That won't be necessary," McMeel says.

One woman says she's played all her life and still shoots in the 120s and 130s. "I have high hopes in this tournament," she says. "I expect to be really, really bad." And you know something, she *was*. She visualized it, then went out and did it.

"I've improved," says a 125-er from Cleveland, "in that I've stopped throwing my clubs—because they're too expensive these days."

Some of the golfers even have physical handicaps, yet remain undeterred. "My instructor said I'm just the wrong size to play," says a burly fella. "He said that at my height and weight he could give me a hundred lessons and I'd never be any good." What an inspiring teacher. So the brawny lad says he saved his money and shoots the same 115 ("not counting all the strokes," and who among us really does?) he would have if he'd spent $10,000 on lessons.

But how do they *feel* about sucking at golf? "It's embarrassing," says one man. "Guys will call and ask my wife to play and say I can come along and carry the bags."

McMeel tells a comforting tale: "I was invited to play at Augusta, where they play the Masters. I was going to rent clubs, but they don't rent [apparently Palmer, Nicklaus, and Woods all have their own]. We played for three days—three of the longest days of my life. At the end of the third day, my host says, 'John, look around, because you're never gonna see this place ever again.' And he meant it. I notice that whenever I'm invited to play golf by someone, they only ask once."

The impressive thing about almost all of these bad

golfers is that they aren't just inexperienced golfers. These are golfers who play quite a bit and are still just god-awful. Never get any better. McMeel is like this, a president who leads by example, consistently and earnestly playing really bad golf that is, frankly, horrifying at times.

In a Bad Golfers Association tournament, is it the low scorer or high scorer who wins? Or is it like high-low poker, where they split the pot. And what is the pot?

On the eve of their national tournament, McMeel and Oliphant seem taken aback by this question. They really haven't thought about it, which seems unusual, since they've thought about everything else—except, the BGA isn't big on score-keeping.

This becomes obvious when one reads "The Rules of Golf—According to the Bad Golfers Association," rules that are rather at odds with the Rules of Golf as written by the USGA.

Take the BGA's definition of par, for example: "Par: The BGA rejects this as an elitist definition which may force BGA members to attempt emulation of ego-driven over-achievers with whom they would never normally or willingly associate. Par, the BGA defines as being whatever you say it is."

Or their definition of "Strokes Taken: The number of strokes a player has taken shall not necessarily include any penalty strokes incurred. In fact, the final score taken should not necessarily include some of the actual strokes taken."

The tournament is to be played in accordance with the BGA rules, so I boned up on the idiosyncrasies the night before. One of the cardinal rules of the BGA is that taking golf lessons is anathema and if you take them you're out. My lessons in the grade school gym, then, would seem to disqualify me! Have I made this pilgrimage to Kansas City in vain? Not necessarily, since the one BGA rule that seems to override all others is that none of these rules apply unless you're caught. It seems to be the ol' "don't ask—don't tell" rule that Bill Clinton put into effect to cover gays in the military and interns under his desk.

Although it remains unclear whether high or low score will win the tournament, I opt to try to beat this gathering of golf klutzes, to try to be best of the worst (the tallest dwarf in the circus), to try to win *something*, to best *somebody*, in this god-forsaken sportlike leisure time activity.

And I am leaving nothing to chance. I procure a secret weapon that I believe will ensure victory: the Ballistic Driver.

Now, Ballistic Driver is more than just a name, more than just another new miracle club fashioned from some revolutionary new super-turbo-titanium amalgamation, more than a driver with a head bigger than Bertha's.

This son-of-a-bitch uses real bullets! Explosives! The clubhead opens up like a rifle chamber, which it is, then a .27 caliber bullet is loaded, and the chamber locked. Then the weapon is placed two inches behind the ball, a trigger on the club grip is pulled, and BLAM! the bullet fires, and the spring-loaded face of the driver shoots forward at two hundred miles per hour, blasting the ball 250 yards! Every time. Without even swinging. Seriously. All you do is line it up.

I talked with the developer of the club, Jim Duncalf,

who told me it doesn't leave a big hole in the ground when it explodes, and isn't even all that loud because it's equipped with a silencer. He agreed to ship one to my hotel in Kansas City, because, after all, you couldn't very well carry the damned thing on an airplane, now could you? Those little security personnel stationed at the airport metal detectors would go . . . ballistic.

Will I need a firearms license to play golf with this contraption? Would there be a three-day waiting period? Background checks? Would they find out about my toll evasion charge on the Tri-State Tollway in Chicago?

"The Ballistic Driver is not a joke," answered Duncalf. "Think how they could help handicapped golfers. Would you like to invest $100,000?" I told him no, and that I really didn't even want to send him $800 for the Driver, so he let me use it free just this one time.

I assured him it was no joke to me either. Anything that would remove my unsightly swing from my golf game was a serious improvement. It sort of reminded me of dynamite fishing in Texas, which consists of lighting a stick of dynamite, tossing it into a lake or stream, and harvesting stunned fish and fish particles. I "caught" some little sunfish once as a kid utilizing this same technique and waterproof cherry bombs. Like dynamite fishing, the Ballistic Driver also bypasses the need for expensive equipment, knowledge, and skill. No permit is needed, since it is not permitted.

Think Chuck Connors meets John Daly. We figured out the little honey in our hotel room, then carried it under wraps to the practice range at the tournament, where I loaded it, cocked it, put it behind the ball, pulled the trigger, and winced.

There was a harmless "click," followed by another and another and another. New bullets didn't help. Rereading the directions didn't help. All it would do was misfire.

(After the tournament I sent the Driver back to the manufacturers. I tried to call them to discuss another try sometime, but the phone was disconnected. Their fax no longer worked. My letters went unanswered. I did some research and read that this was not the first time the Ballistic Driver had failed during a public demonstration.)

I was crushed. I would have to try to win this thing "legitimately," if you will.

The Ballistic Driver was just like everything else I tried to improve my golf game: It didn't work.

I am placed in an esteemed (here, at least) foursome, with President McMeel, titular vice president Oliphant, and their buddy, John O'Day, who is a complete gentleman and a good golfer, all of which means he has absolutely no business being in this tournament. If he wins the tournament with low score I'll be filing a protest with the commissioner. How can they allow this . . . golfer! . . . into this tournament.

Luckily, a tournament sponsor provides golf shoes to every contestant, because I don't have mine. I really like the clicking sound the spikes make as I tread the walkways. Feel like a real golfer. I have worn them once since, and had to take them to the pro shop to be refitted with the mandatory, new soft rubber spikes that make no racket and are no fun at all.

Luckily, they're renting clubs, because I don't have any of those either. Probably I would do a lot better if I had a $2,000 set of custom-made clubs, but it is still unclear to me whether I want to hit the ball farther or not until I get the whole directional thing worked out.

The "golfers" board their carts, Indy 500–style, and hear a man with a bullhorn bellow: "Good luck and bad golf to all!" There is a little bumper cart action as sixty-six carts scatter to their assigned tees.

John McMeel drives me to the first tee, where he pencils in our names on the scorecard. Everyone else has short little golf pencils, but his is long, with an eraser. "All the better to make necessary adjustments," he explained. So . . . *he* will be scoring—a potentially decisive advantage.

Pat and John O'Day arrive, and it's time to tee off. They're suspicious of me. I talk a bad game, sure, but you know it's not enough to simply talk a bad game—there comes a moment in time when you have to tee it up and prove yourself on the field of play. And I will, time and time again, in the sands, the groves, and the ravines here at this country club.

We go over a mental checklist, like pilots readying for takeoff:

"Plenty of paramedics on hand?" I ask.

"Check," replies McMeel.

"Chainsaws, shovels, machetes?" queries Oliphant.

Check.

"Trailerful of balls?"

Check.

"Scorecard already filled out for all 18 holes?" Oliphant asks McMeel.

Suspiciously, no answer.

"Beverage cart operational?" Oliphant asks with a serious note of concern.

Check.

They want me to tee off first, but we have to wait for a foursome ahead of us, which is taking a little of the pressure off me by hitting some astonishingly ghastly drives.

"Wait for the laughter to die down," McMeel advises, "then you can go." Say what you will, McMeel *knows* bad golf etiquette.

And, of course, bad golf etiquette requires your partners not to be quiet when you're lining up a shot, but rather to advise and encourage you. As I stand over my first drive, McMeel compliments me on my "matching outfit," clearly just trying to distract me because my outfit is purposely mismatched owing to my complete disdain for those cute cabana sets some golfers wear.

"Don't think about the trees," Oliphant says helpfully.

"Could you guys be quiet for a second?" I plead.

"Bill, Bill, Bill," chides McMeel, walking over and opening the BGA rule book. "This is covered right here in the BGA rule book."

And, indeed, there it is, right there on page 5, Section I-2: "Consideration for Other Players: When a player is addressing the ball or making a stroke, the general atmosphere of camaraderie is enhanced when other players stand close behind and talk to each other, and make disparaging remarks concerning that player's ability."

I should have remembered my Walkman. I swing away,

hitting the ball rather nicely, except for the sharp right it seems to be taking.

"Do you see it?" I ask. I never see where my drives go. I think it's because I really don't *want* to know.

"Yes," answers McMeel.

"It's on the fairway," says Oliphant.

"Just not *our* fairway," adds O'Day. "Please try again."

Now here is a group of good Christian athletes, who will give a guy a little down on his luck a second chance— unlike most of the uncharitable bastards who play this game.

My second drive is better: shorter, in the rough, next to a stand of trees and probably even findable.

"You're in the shade," cheers McMeel, "which is good. It's a hot one today."

I step back, standing ready now myself to helpfully offer advice and encouragement to my golfing partners.

"Don't even think about the crowd of people watching, here, Johnny," Oliphant says, as McMeel steps to the tee. His first two tee shots go . . . somewhere. His third lands near mine.

Pat hits his drive farther than we did, right in the center of the fairway, but not *this* fairway. He decides to play it from there, however, as it is not all that far—as the crow flies—from the intended green.

O'Day hits a painfully beautiful drive, but it hits a rock or sprinkler head or something and bounces almost sideways into the rough.

To speed things up—can you even *imagine* how long it would take the 132 worst golfers in America to play 18 holes?—this is a "best ball" tournament, which means the four of us each take our second shots from wherever the best of our four first shots landed. However, on the opening drive, none of us had hit even a *good* shot, let alone a *best* shot, so maybe we should be playing "better ball" or "least bad ball" or maybe here in the BGA tournament we should be playing "worst ball." Best ball for our foursome meant that in almost every case we'd be hitting our next shots from wherever O'Day's previous shot landed.

McMeel hits his second shot. Five feet. He hits his third shot. Ten feet. I figured everyone had just been giving him a hard time about his game, but you know something? John McMeel is every bit as bad as people say he is.

In keeping with BGA etiquette, McMeel's lame shots are met with Oliphant's loud guffaws. "It's the ground crew's fault," McMeel snaps. "If they'd mown the rough instead of the fairways, we'd be fine."

To fit in, I hit my second shot ten feet. I seem to be playing down to the level of the competition, and they like that.

"Beautiful form though, Bill," McMeel comments, at once politely and impolitely.

Pat is over on the other fairway behind the trees having his way with his ball, as O'Day hits his second shot distressingly well. It rolls to the edge of the green, but then somehow rolls back into the sand trap. Tough luck.

There is a sponsor sign on the sand trap. Unlike other tournaments, the *holes* are not sponsored here, the *hazards* are. Because that's where most of the action takes place. By the 18th hole the sand traps should have been sponsored by Dr. Jack Kevorkian.

O'Day blasts out of the sand—on his first try!—to within five feet of the pin. Then McMeel takes his S wedge and begins flailing away at the sand, like a dog going after a buried T-bone or perhaps a cat trying to cover up something in a litter box. After his fourth whack at it, he picks up his ball and carries it out of the sand.

With scores already soaring, my partners are beginning to take things into their own hands.

"Let me show you the art of bunker play," Pat says to me, as he steps into the sand: "First of all, you wait till everyone else is up on the green, so all they can see is the top of your head, then you take the ball and some sand in your left hand, swing your club, and release the ball and the sand during your swing, letting the ball and the sand fly onto the green."

He demonstrates as I watch from the green. He makes a perfect toss that rolls within inches of the hole, and from my vantage point it looks like Tiger himself has stroked it.

"Good out!" yells McMeel.

"But isn't that, you know . . . *cheating?*" I ask.

"No, no, no, Bill, please," says McMeel. "We don't like to call it 'cheating.' Our creed or credo or whatever, is that if you can get away with it you can do anything: We don't like to call it cheating—a compromise, maybe, or self-help. Anyway that shot is covered in the rule book."

And, indeed, there it is, right on page 29: "Relief Situations: The ball may be lifted and resituated. . . . When the player has been unable to hit the ball over the overhanging rim of a sand trap, the player may pick up the ball and a handful of sand and launch both as far as possible toward the pin. The sand lends authenticity and should head off imprudent questions."

Okay, so I try it. But my shot isn't nearly as graceful or believable or close to the hole. In golf, even cheating well takes practice.

John O'Day sinks his putt, so our team takes a 4 on the first hole. "Couldn't the other three of us just head on back to the clubhouse?" I ask. "I'm not sure I understand our function out here playing 'best ball'? Can't O'Day just do this himself?" Yet we play on.

On the second tee, I fail to hit the ball as far as the ladies' tee and Oliphant immediately whips out the rule book. He turns to page 17, and tries to invoke the rule whereby "a male player having not, on his initial drive, hit his ball beyond the ladies' tee shall complete that hole with his 'membership' hanging out." Fortunately, mulligans were on sale at the tournament for $25 and McMeel buys me one, explaining: "Nobody wants to see that." I tell him I haven't seen it for a while myself without the aid of a dental mirror. Not that I need it, it's just nice to know it's still there.

After the second shot on the second hole, we three dingbats are wandering the woods on the right side of the fairway—slicers, all—in search of our (golf) balls. Oliphant shows me the rule book's definition of: "Lost Ball: A ball is 'lost' if you have decided the terrain does not warrant screwing with it. If the ball is actually found in such terrain it can be quietly booted into the next county and another put down without penalty in more hospitable surroundings. If the ball is actually lost . . . the same solution applies."

There are nuances: "It is sometimes profitable for a player to assist another player in the search for his or her ball. If the assisting player should find the ball first, that player may find it possible to pocket the ball without attracting undue attention and . . . the [other] player will then have to put down another ball for a one-stroke penalty."

"Here's your ball," he says, handing me my ball. "I'll give you a break this time, since you're a novice." Truly a babe in the woods. So much to learn from these masters. I notice that Oliphant always speeds ahead in his golf cart to take command of the situation, and I start riding with him. My scores improve immediately. He has found ways to improve his game without costly equipment and lessons.

"Found mine!" he yells, discreetly dropping a new ball on the edge of the fairway.

"Me, too!" calls out McMeel, whose ball, believe it or not, is also on the fairway. How fortunate.

Pat instructs me that when playing with straight-arrow sticklers it's sometimes necessary to be deft of hand to disguise the fact that you are dropping another ball. He's the one who advises cutting a hole in my right front pants pocket and dropping the ball down through it rather than tossing a ball or stooping over to put one down—both of which arouse suspicion.

At the next tee some absolute *fool* is trying to sell chances to win airline tickets if we hit a hole-in-one. We all have a good chuckle over that. (There is such a thing as "hole-in-one insurance," whereby a tournament offers, say, a $100,000 prize for a hole-in-one and buys insurance based on the hole distance, number of players in the tournament, and so forth. So, the insurance premium for, say, a $1 million prize on a two-hundred-yard hole at the BGA tournament would probably run about what? Five bucks?) At another hole, golfers could, theoretically, win a new Buick for a hole-in-one. If you're in the market for a late-model Buick that's never been driven, it's probably still sitting there.

Over the course of the next couple of holes, I notice an odd thing happening—a great thing: O'Day isn't always hitting the best ball. Sometimes even *I* do. In golf, we what? *Learn from one another!* Bad golf is contagious.

"John O'Day was a fine golfer until he met us," McMeel explains.

"I used to be a 16 handicap," O'Day confirms, "then I went to 20, played with these guys a few more times and went to a 24, and today I'm probably a 30 thanks to them."

On the next tee, I whiff, missing the ball completely. Luckily BGA rules read: "These swings shall be deemed practice swings and are not subject to penalty . . . intent to hit the ball is immaterial and cannot be proven anyway."

I swing again, hitting my ball about three feet on my second try, ten feet on my third, and next elect to *throw* not the ball, but rather my driver. Just five feet or so, but the head comes off, which makes driving just that much more difficult the rest of the day. There is laughing. You never see laughing at PGA tournaments. Even my throwing is critiqued: "Use more of a helicopter motion rather than just the straight toss," Oliphant suggests, sounding like he knows whereof he speaks.

At televised PGA events you don't see members of the ground crew aerating the greens, removing big plugs, with a machine, *while you're putting*. I don't think we were being taken seriously. You don't see dogs copulating on the course on TV either, but you do here.

On the next hole, my drive lands on the fairway—hurrah!—and bounces just barely into the rough. O'Day's drive is on the fairway, but not as close to the hole as mine. Mine has a chance of being best ball! Oliphant rushes me to the scene in his cart.

"Your ball has an *awkward* lie," he proclaims.

"If a ball has an awkward lie, you can *adjust* it?" I ask.

"Yes," Pat says, "with your feet and hands. You can just toss it to a better spot, although kicking is not as noticeable." Without even looking, this BGA pro nonchalantly and adroitly gives my ball two short kicks, soccer-style, out of the rough onto the fairway.

McMeel arrives: "This is why Pat is known on the golf course as 'The Tailor.' He's a master craftsman at making alterations and adjustments, shortening, lengthening, moving, letting it out a little." And I must say, he certainly had tailored my rather unsightly shot into "best ball"!

The next fairway has a big lake right in the middle of it. McMeel explains to me the physics of golf balls and water, and the ongoing battery of scientific tests concerning the propensity of water to exert a gravitational pull on golf balls, thereby pulling them down into the water in a most dastardly fashion.

"Until those tests are completed," he explains, "the BGA allows golfers to place a provisional ball on the other side of water hazards without penalty."

So trying to drive over the water was just for fun, didn't count. Possibly because it isn't necessary, I do in fact hit my drive over the water in complete dryness. So does O'Day, of course, followed by McMeel, who sees two perfect drives sucked down by that unexplained pull.

"Do you have a snorkel in your golf bag?" asks Oliphant. "A rubber raft?"

Then he steps up and executes the shot of the day. Pat puts a little something extra into his tee shot in an attempt to clear the lake. His ball blasts off at a low angle, hits the water, but skips twice on the surface, and carries to dry land, where it hits a tree, ricochets off a fence, hits a golf cart, shoots straight toward a TV crew covering the tournament, scatters them, and plops back into the water.

We stand in stunned silence. Finally, McMeel speaks for us all: "*That,* is the shot of the day!" Best I'd seen. Ever. The three of us break into applause.

"Do I get the Buick?" Oliphant cries. McMeel says, "No, but you're up for the Gerald Ford Public Safety Award."

Possibly owing to shots like that, the galleries are smaller than I'd expected at a national tournament. Apparently they were bigger last year, but many fans are still out with injuries. Two women sitting on a bench by the next tee say that they sometimes find it necessary to get behind or under the bench.

The day is peppered with shouts of "Fore!" "Watch out!" "Duck!" "Hit the dirt!" "We surrender!" "Hey, asshole!" and the like, as these bad golfers spray the course with errant shots. Word is that a squirrel has been killed or perhaps just coldcocked by one such shot. The course isn't safe for man nor beast.

"If you hit anybody or anything," advises Oliphant, "it's best to leave the area as quickly as you can." He carries a collection of other people's business cards so that if he does any damage he can express his regrets and leave the card so they can contact "him" should there be medical or repair bills. As the rule book clearly states: "The BGA believes that litigation has no place in the game of golf. Any maneuver employed to protect the reputation of the game and its adherents is to be applauded."

O'Day tells of breaking the windshield of a car once with one of his shots and his stunned partners looking at him and asking, "What are you going to do?" To which he replied: "I think I'll change my grip a tad, maybe rotate my hands a quarter inch on my next try."

The next hole is 592 friggin' yards. "Can't be!" wails Oliphant. "Did you bring something to eat? We'll need a picnic basket." We tee off, hop into his cart, and set out to find our balls. When we come upon his—in the fairway!—instead of stopping the cart he leans out, snatches his ball on the move, and gives it a cart ride another hundred yards. We dub this "taxiing" the ball to the green. From the moving cart he tosses it onto the green, with great accuracy. Very impressive, but you have to remember that he's been cheating a long, long time.

This elongated hole—a third of a mile!—takes forever, after which we're so tired we decide to skip the next hole. We are encouraged to do this by the course starter, who makes a special trip out from the clubhouse to tell us we're playing too slowly. He is obviously unfamiliar with BGA rules: "Golf is not a game to be hurried. Therefore never allow another group to play through."

On the next hole, the green abuts a narrow street with houses just on the other side. I hit a ball too hard, over the fence, over the street, and over a house.

"Hear that?" shouts Oliphant. "I think I heard the ping of a Weber grill in that guy's backyard." I can't try to retrieve it as there is barbed wire on the top of the fence surrounding the course, which I think has less to do with keeping interlopers out of the exclusive club and more to do with keeping BGA golfers in. I drop a new ball by the fence.

"Oh, you found your ball," says Oliphant. "Any barbecue sauce on it?"

As I try to putt, my partners continue to advise and encourage me, jingle change in their pockets, and say, "There go those two dogs again." Not to mention, someone drives the cart onto the green itself, parking it between my ball and the hole. I offer sportingly to putt beneath the cart, but am told that, even by BGA rules, the cart must be moved to another spot on the green.

By the 16th hole, we're all dragging, and the gimmee putts grow longer and longer. We're getting a tad surly. I am roundly criticized for not keeping my shots close enough to the cart track, thereby taking up too much time and energy. On the 17th green Pat suggests, "Let's not putt," and all four of us pick up our balls and move on. "Whose big idea was 18 holes anyway?" someone asks, and we decide to just skip 18 altogether.

It's going to be tough to score this round, but skipping two holes is still one of the quickest ways I know to take

15 strokes off your game. But where do we stand? Has McMeel made up the scores yet? Who won?

Back at the clubhouse everyone is boasting about how badly they played. But who is bad*est?* Who is Worst-Of-Field? Is it McMeel, or Pat, or me, or someone else? I'm not even sure I'm the worst in our foursome. One thing is certain: The future is bright for the BGA, what with McMeel and Oliphant leading the way and more and more bad golfers taking up the game every day.

Scores are difficult to calculate, what with the various ball adjustments and skipping holes and such. And no one ever seemed to be writing anything down. "Would you?" asks McMeel.

I figure O'Day shot somewhere in the high 80s, plus the two holes we skipped, giving him about a 97. McMeel, Oliphant, and I were at about 115, plus the throws, kicks, penalty strokes, and those skipped holes, which puts us at right about the 135 mark. But that great shot of Pat's: skipping off the water, into a tree, a fence, a cart, nearly killing members of a TV crew, then back into the water—well, that sort of took the cake. I'm not taking anything away from myself, I'm not saying I'm not as bad or worse than he is, I'm just saying that this day he has been just *sensationally* atrocious.

And, there are rumors that some guy is in the clubhouse, atop the leader board (or buried somewhere beneath it), with a legitimate 188! Extraordinary. The man has almost shot his weight.

Who is the absolute worst? Who is the best of the worst? Who knows? But in the Bad Golfers Association tournament, it can truly be said that there are no winners,

Bill Geist

that everyone here is a loser—and that's the beautiful thing.

"You've proven that you belong here among the nation's elite bad golfers," President McMeel says to me at the closing ceremonies—and he does offer to give me a sash proclaiming me the worst in my state.

Unfortunately, with this array of talent, not everyone can lose. This day, I am not the worst golfer in the world, and I am not the best of the worst. I am nothing. Not to mention, a guy from the pro shop shows up with a bill for $300 to replace the club I'd beheaded.

At golf, I just can't win.

EPILOGUE

Still Par Free

At this point, after spending many months at the game, I realize that I still haven't purchased clubs. This may be a measure of my commitment. I haven't bought clubs and I haven't joined any. I haven't shopped for golf attire and I haven't been asked back by anyone to play a second time.

I believe I have definitely improved, although my scores don't reflect this. After my lessons, and using my wife's good clubs, I can hit the ball straighter more often. And do I ever hit it more often. But still not very far. I've developed into a consistently bad golfer—rather than a spectacularly horrendous one. Golf seems to take time, effort, and dedication—and isn't that too bad?

I have developed something akin to respect for good golfers and a better appreciation of the game. I kind of like to watch it on TV, although I didn't really need another reason to vegetate in front of the set, now did I?

And I can now chat about golf with friends at parties: "Olazabel faded a 3-iron 225 to the apron, no bite, dead within the leather—rub of the green." Abso-friggin'-lutely!

As for my future in golf, I am troubled by a recent court ruling in my home state of New Jersey that held liable an inexperienced golfer like myself who was playing on a public course and hit a partner in his foursome with his tee shot. Deeply troubled. The victim was sitting in a golf cart ten or fifteen feet ahead of the tee at about a 45 degree angle when the novice hooked one. The hittee thought he was safe because the guy had just sliced his first tee shot. This is an all too familiar pattern. So, on the advice of my golf attorneys, until and unless that appellate ruling is overturned, I really can't afford to continue.

And besides, I'm still not quite sure I like golf. I like the carts and the cocktails and the idea that even in my "middle age" (middle of some serious decay) there is a "sport" in which I could possibly still improve. I do like the landscaping, the rare serenity in this day and age, the escape, and most of all the camaraderie. I've had some great fun playing amongst terribly witty terrible golfers.

As for what we're actually out here *doing* with all this waggery, this beauty, this tranquillity, this bonhomie—struggling with this maddening addiction in an attempt to reach the impossible par . . . well, I'm still not quite sure I get it.